Give Yourself A Number

The
CUSTOMER LOYALTY
Advantage

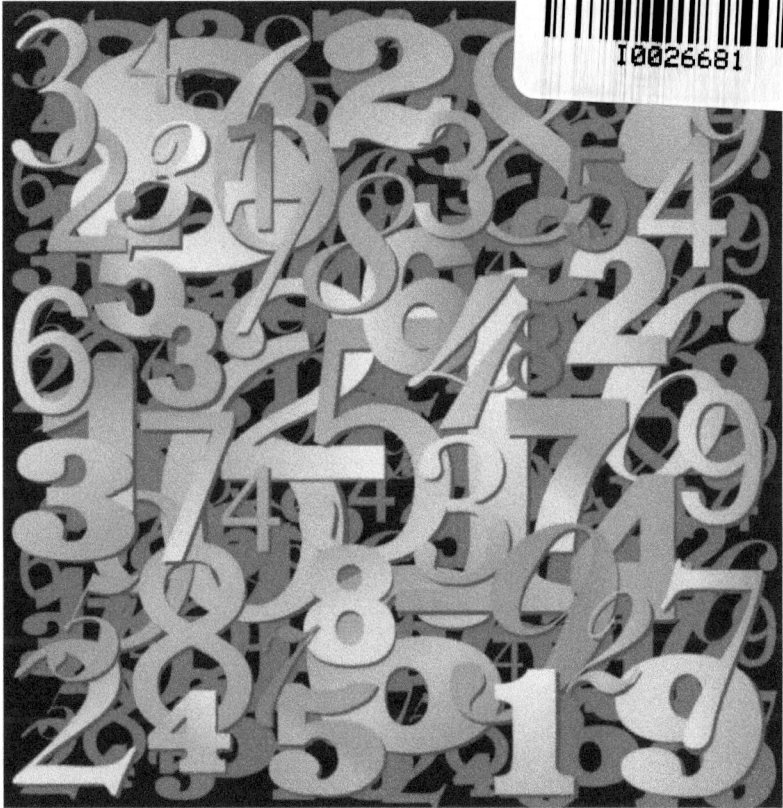

'How' to Create Customer Loyalty

"Want better customer outcomes?
It's as easy as counting to 10"

A book by Dennis Koci

Published by Hospitality Performance Management Publishing, Los Angeles, California

Images used under license from Shutterstock.com

For questions, comments or to order bulk quantities, contact: info@giveyourselfanumber.com

Printed in the United States of America
First Edition

ISBN-13: 978-1-7328899-1-0 (HPM Publishing)

Dedication

To Wayne, who throughout his life, demonstrated how to be the best son, brother, husband, father, grandfather and friend to those close to him, and whom I've admired since the day I met him.

Table of Contents

PART II: CUSTOMER LOYALTY

PART III: THE GYAN PROCESS

Preface

I don't know your organization, business, or industry, and the challenges you face, as well as you do. But I do know the hotel business, where, instead of a physical product, the only thing you have after you leave, besides a bill, is thoughts of what you experienced during your stay. You have a 'feeling' about your comfort, an assessment of the ability of our facility and staff to allow you to accomplish the purpose of your visit, and the memory of that experience. And, how well your stay experience was, is largely a result of the 'customer service' the hotel staff provided.

I have the highest respect for the men and women that work in the service business. It can be one of the most fulfilling and rewarding careers on the planet. And when what you do as an employee can affect how another person feels, that gives you an idea of how really important customer service can be. Imagine leaving your hotel room, heading for the elevator, and being greeted with a smile and a cheerful hello from a housekeeper that you passed in the corridor. It can brighten your day.

You may have to define it very broadly, but every organization, including yours, has 'customers.' And you know that the Customer Experience (CX) is important to the success of your business, but how important? According to customer research done by Gartner Inc. in 2017, 89% of markets expect customer experience to be their primary differentiator when deciding to become a customer. Their research also showed CX to be the single biggest opportunity for improving organizational results in 2017.[1]

So, what makes up the customer experience? Customer experience is defined by interactions between a customer and an organization throughout their business relationship. An interaction can include awareness, discovery, service, and value received. Customer service, (along with Customer Experience-CX, Customer Relationship Management-CRM, Customer Experience Management-CEM), may be some of the most talked about topics in business today. And, everyone agrees they're important.

The problem for an owner or manager, is that you cannot personally be there all the time and at all the various touch-points where the customer interacts with your organization. You'd like to make every one of your customers feel welcome, let them know that you care about them and know that you are responsive to their needs, and engage with them throughout their entire customer experience with your organization, but you can't. You must rely on your team; employees[2] in Marketing, Web Design, Support Centers, Sales, Operations, etc., to help you with that. And how well the Customer's Experience is while interacting with your organization, will determine your organization's success. If that's true, I began to wonder where someone might go, if they needed help further improving the customer experience they provide.

So, before I began to write this book, I did a search for 'Customer Service' on Amazon Books and found that there were over 10,000 books on the topic. So, while Customer Service is critical to the success of any organization, it seems like it has been so completely covered and discussed, that there was nothing else to add. But I noticed something as I scanned some of the book reviews. While most everyone enjoyed reading the various books, there seemed to be one recurring theme. There was general consensus that the author understood the topic and explained it well. But after they finished reading the book, it was hard for the reader to verbalize what specifically they would do with the information. They couldn't explain 'how' to turn the information from these experts, into specific actions.

According to public data published by the American Customer Satisfaction Index (www.theacsi.org), overall customer satisfaction is about where it was four years ago (4Q2013: 76.8 vs 4Q2017: 76.7). And Arizona State University's School of Business in it's biannual 'Customer Rage' survey for 2017, found that incidences of problems experienced have increased to 56%, an all-time high. Further, of those that complained, 79% were still not happy with the way their complaints were handled.[3] So, while these 10,000+ books haven't dampened anyone's enthusiasm for the topic, they may not have had the positive impact that was their intention. The reason may be that most customer service advice focuses on 'what to do' but not 'how to do it.' So, instead of specifics, you might hear organizations provide vague pronouncements, such as: 'Our goal is to create a truly incredible Customer Service organization,' or 'We're putting the Customer First', or 'Make customer service Priority One' or other similar end-result statements. It's all well intended and it sounds good, but 'how'? What specifically needs to be done, to make every staff member understand 'how' to accomplish the goal of, say, incredible customer service, when they face an infinite number of customers and situations?

My goal in sharing this book with you, is to try to clearly explain not only what you and your team can do to improve customer service, but 'how' to do it, with a process that will allow everyone to self-evaluate their own unique customer interactions, and chose the one that yields the best customer outcome. And from that point of clarity, I hope that whether you are the owner, a manager, supervisor, or front-line customer contact employee just starting out, you will receive at least one idea, concept or notion that you can implement, that will improve the experiences of those you consider 'customers.'

If I'm successful, it will not only change the way you look at customer service, but will have a positive impact on the employees and the customers with whom you interact… and maybe even society as a whole.

-Dennis Koci, Los Angeles-January, 2019.

Introduction

The book is organized into three parts: Part I and II describe the fundamentals of Customer Satisfaction and Customer Loyalty, and Part III introduces the Give Yourself A Number (GYAN) Process.

It's been emphasized, that being able to satisfy customers is fundamental to the success of any organization. That's why the focus of Part I of the book is on Customer Satisfaction: what it is, how is it measured and how it is delivered.

Part II will describe the concept of Customer Loyalty, and while Customer Satisfaction is a necessary component, the other factors used in determining Customer Loyalty are discussed and explained. Then the process of how Customers decide to become loyal is reviewed, along with a discussion on common barriers that may interfere with an organization's ability to capture and maintain their Customer's loyalty.

Part II concludes with a chapter on how Customer Loyalty is impacted when things go wrong, and the opportunity that problems and complaints present, to not only resolve the immediate customer issues, but to further increase and strengthen future Customer Loyalty.

With an understanding of the inter-relationship between Customer Satisfaction and Customer Loyalty to build upon, we'll have a good idea of what every organization needs to focus on that has Customer Loyalty as their goal. But knowing 'what' your goal is, for example, improving customer's positive experiences, is only part of it.

It's the 'how' that is the challenging part for most of the Customer Relationship/Experience Management literature, when attempting to offer advice on achieving the goal of Customer Loyalty.

The reason why most Customer Loyalty advice is hard to put into action is that every customer, and every situation, is potentially unique. So, the same things that satisfy one customer may not satisfy the next. Even the things that satisfied the same customer last time, may not satisfy them this time. And, if responses are 'scripted' or a standardized approach is used for consistency, it will satisfy some customers, but not all.

In my experience, what is needed is a real-time process, unique to the current specific customer situation, that creates and improves Customer Loyalty. And, it must be simple for everyone in the entire organization to understand, and use. That's what the 'Give yourself A Number' (GYAN) Customer Loyalty process in Part III of the book, is designed to do.

The GYAN Process is different from the information found in typical customer service training sessions. It allows for self-evaluation of employee/customer situations in real-time, providing a framework that you can use in every situation with every customer, leading to the highest Customer satisfaction and loyalty result.

So, as you read Part I and II of the book, reflect on the Customer Satisfaction and Customer Loyalty issues that currently face you and your organization, and the changes and improvements you'd like to make. Then in Part III, following the GYAN introduction, use the examples cited and the templates provided, to help put your thoughts and ideas into action. As you review the GYAN process you may even consider and re-evaluate how you currently coach and train your staff.

Throughout the book, I refer to 'you' or 'your organization.' This is to give every reader a 360° view of the multiple perspectives involved. Sometimes it refers to the customer service employee/service provider, and at other times it's as if the reader was the owner or manager of a business, and even you as a customer. But it doesn't matter where you are on your company's organization chart, or even if you are just starting out in customer service, reading this book can help you. It's a process that helps anyone in customer service (that's all of us), self-evaluate the situation and make mid-course corrections if necessary, to get to the best customer outcome. That's what the GYAN Process is designed to do.

Now you know. Now it's up to you.

PART I

CUSTOMER SATISFACTION

Chapter 1: Defining Customer Satisfaction

What is Customer Satisfaction, Anyway?

An article published in the *Academy of Marketing Science Review*, stated that: "A review of the existing literature indicates a wide variance in the definitions of satisfaction. The lack of a consensus definition limits the contribution of consumer satisfaction research. Without a uniform definition of satisfaction, researchers are unable to select an appropriate definition for a given context; develop valid measures of satisfaction; and/or compare and interpret empirical results."[4]

While there is no shortage of attempts to explain it, the inability to define a concept often considered vital to the success of a business, may be the reason there is so little actionable advice on the subject. And, the reason it's difficult to deliver consistent excellent customer service is not only that few know what it is, but even fewer know 'how' to provide it, consistently.

Even customer experts agree it's a difficult challenge. Here's what the Marketing Science Institute, an organization dedicated to bridging the gap between academic marketing theory and business practice has said: "Customer loyalty is the most important goal of marketers, but achieving loyalty and reaping its rewards remain ongoing challenges." And Shep Hyken, a customer service expert and bestselling author has said: "Over the years, I've written that to create customer loyalty, you must focus on two things: customer service and creating confidence. The combination of those two gives you *a shot* [emphasis added] at creating customer loyalty."[5]

When approaching customer service training, some say the solution to customer satisfaction, is to use a *consistent approach*. It's a common training method, as customer service manuals and guidelines train customer service agents to memorize 'scripted' responses to typical customer requests. But, if what's wanted is a *consistent outcome*, then a consistent approach won't work, as each customer is potentially unique. If we want a consistent positive outcome with customers, it will take a process that can be customized to allow for each unique interaction between the customer and each customer service provider to be created and self-evaluated in real time, in order to come up with the optimum customer outcome. That's what this book will attempt to do, but let's not get ahead of ourselves. Let's try to get to the bottom of this dilemma by developing a basic understanding of customer satisfaction 'the what,' and then explore 'how' to get the best outcome. Let's start with a general definition.

At any particular moment and at the most basic level, customer satisfaction equals the service level the customer actually received *from the customer's perspective*, minus the customer's expectation of the service level they desired/anticipated they would receive. It can be positive, negative, or neutral. To represent it as an equation:

Customer Satisfaction = Service level received (or Product utility received) – Expectations

But customer satisfaction is not as simple as it looks. If it were, everyone would be satisfying their customers every time, and they don't. We will use this working definition going forward and briefly discuss its measurement. Then in later chapters, we will explore the real question: 'how' to deliver it at the highest positive level, using the GYAN (Give Yourself A Number) process.

Customer Satisfaction: How are we doing?

Accenture's 2013 Global Consumer Pulse Survey found that customers are increasingly frustrated with the level of services they experience: 91 percent of respondents are frustrated that they have to contact a company multiple times for the same reason; 90 percent mentioned being put on hold for a long time, and 89 percent mentioned having to repeat their issue to multiple representatives.[6]

Part of the reason for the frustration, is because with improvements in technology and competitive innovations, customer expectations are also increasing. And, at the same time, companies, striving to reduce overhead expenses, cut back on staffing and training expenses.

In the hotel industry, J.D. Power reported that overall satisfaction with the guest experience declined, partly due to rising customer expectations. They found that 18% of respondents indicated that they had a problem during their stay. Problem occurrence can have a strong negative impact on overall guest satisfaction. Satisfaction among guests that experienced a problem during their stay averaged more than 100 points lower (on a scale maximum of 1,000) than those guests with a problem-free experience.[7] There also seems to be a general lack of recognition by the staff about the opportunity created, when a customer reports a problem. (For more on the discussion on how to use reported problems to actually increase customer loyalty, see the discussion on 'Complaints are your Friend,' later in the book).

What about looking at the companies that are the best in customer service? The 2016 *Zogby Analytics, 24/7 Wall St.* survey, dubbed 'The Customer Service Hall of Fame," surveyed customer respondents of over 150 of the largest U.S. companies in terms of sales in customer facing industries. The authors then ranked the companies in terms of customer service reported as: Excellent, Good, Fair, and Poor. *Amazon* topped the list, followed by *Chick-fil-A, Apple, Marriott, Samsung, Sony, Google, Netflix, FedEx, UPS, YouTube, American Express, Hilton, and Starbucks.* But even for the customer service winner at the top of the list, only 61.2% of the respondents rated them excellent.[8]

Think about that. The 'Best' American company in terms of customer service is rated excellent by only 61.2% of its customers. Number 2 had an excellent score of 48.9%. This tells us a few things. First, with all the customer service 'experts' out there, no one has figured out the mystery of providing consistently *excellent* customer service. Second, there is a huge opportunity for you and your employees to become better than the best.

What was perhaps more surprising, was how these successful companies explained how they got to be one of the best companies in terms of customer service. When companies that ranked high in customer satisfaction were each asked what their secrets were, responses included: 'We put our customers before profits.' Others cited: 'Having a friendly and knowledgeable staff,' and 'an emphasis on convenience.' Also mentioned: Having a 'customer obsession' as a guiding core principle.

Sounds like all good things. But when you think about it, either as a manager at one of these well-run companies, or as an employee, other than a general impression of what is expected, their explanation offers very little guidance to the oftentimes very specific nature of a customer request or complaint.

What about: "If you treat your employees well, they will treat the customer well"? It's always a good idea to treat employees[9] well. After all, they are an important part of your company's success. They see more customers than you do, and they represent you and your company/brand when you're not around.

But as good an idea it is to treat employees well, sadly not every company or supervisor does. And if you do treat the staff well, there is no guarantee that they will pass it on to the customer. It's also not always true that 'happy employees make for happy customers,' something else you may have heard, but didn't understand what it really meant or how to use it.

Is the solution 'Jargonistic Exhortations'?

Ever found yourself along with your colleagues nodding in agreement to what your CEO is saying, but not really knowing what, specifically, they are talking about?   Well, then you've experienced Jargonistic Exhortation. Take for example: "We Need to Focus on Excellence." Sounds good and no one will argue with it, but when the cheers and the glow of the moment is gone, and you're back on the job, do you really now know what to do differently to carry out your new mandate?

Most customer-oriented leadership training is full of these expressions. Ever heard any of the following: 'The customer is our most important asset.' 'The customer is King/Queen.' 'We would be nothing without our customers.' And books giving advice aren't much better. Take for example: 'Determine what training your staff will need in order to become customer-focused and how to do it.' If you didn't know what to do before, you still don't.

What's so wrong about a CEO saying: 'We need to focus on excellence'? Simple critical thinking on the part of the listener, will expose it as meaningless and non-actionable.

Here are other examples:

- "When these goals are met…" or, "…we look forward to future successes."[10]
- "From now on, our team is going to be customer oriented and results driven."
- "Knowing what to do, why it needed to be done, and having the persistence and courage to do it helped leaders turn knowledge…into action."[11]

These expressions are like the familiar weight-loss adage: 'You should burn more calories than you consume.' They are all examples of statements that everyone agrees with, but nobody actually knows 'how' to use them in their everyday situations. Want more? 'Do the right things right.' 'We want 'happy customers, every time.' 'Put the customer at the center of everything we do.' 'Excellent customer service can help retain customers.'   'I'm gonna start running this operation like a business.' 'The key to success is having a well-conceived approach that anticipates problems that are likely to occur.' 'Low hanging fruit, move the needle, raise the bar, structured, yet flexible.' You get the idea. But behavioral improvements that result? Zero.

These well-intended phrases are designed to show how customer focused and enlightened the company, and the company's training process is, while giving everyone the impression that they are showing true leadership. The recipient, usually the employee attending the training class, is in total awe and agreement, but they still don't know what 'new' actions to take to further improve customer service.

So, be aware and try to recognize well-intended but unhelpful jargon. Here's how an executive recently described their company's customer-centric philosophy: "She does whatever she feels makes the most sense to treat the customer with respect and dignity. We have been purposeful about not writing procedures and policies. We treat our customers as we would like to be treated…"[12]

Is the answer, don't even write customer service policies and procedures? In some convoluted world, if you can't describe what you want your customer contact staff to deliver, offering no procedures or policies might sound reasonable. But trusting that your employee will "do the right thing" can lead to disappointment. And in my experience, offering some actionable guidance is more helpful than not doing so.

Is the answer to customer service to follow 'The Golden Rule?' That is, to treat every customer like you would want to be treated? It sounds good, but actually, most customers would like to be treated like *they* want to be treated, not how the customer service employee would like to be treated.

Then there's Nordstrom®, renowned for its great customer service, with 67,000 employees and $12 billion in annual sales. "Throughout their history, they have consistently provided some of the best service in the industry," says Robin Lewis, CEO of *The Robin Report* a Retail Trade publication. Their secret? Nordstrom spokesperson Dan Evans, when discussing their employee handbook, told *Business Insider*: "Our employee handbook is a single card that says "Use good judgment in all situations."[13] Really? Leave customer service up to every employee's 'good judgment?' What if some have it and some don't? Turns out to be a Customer Service myth, according to a 2016 article in *Forbes*[14], where the line, "Use your best judgment" is not on a single card, but just part of Nordstrom's 7,000+ word: 'Code of Business Conduct and Ethics' (May 2017).

I get the impression that these companies know they are successful, but they have a hard time articulating the 'how' of their customer satisfaction success.

Business jargon is sometimes part of the problem in defining customer satisfaction. It is often used to cover-up for the leader who doesn't know what to do, and hopes the employees in the audience will figure it out on their own. At first glance, these statements from management are designed to motivate and inspire. But in the harsh reality of real-time customer interaction, they tend to serve no real purpose. And most of the time, the speakers at the customer service training session do know what they mean to say, they just don't know how to explain it in a way that the employee will not only get what they mean, but they'll know what to do at the right time. Usually, despite management's best intentions, the employee that interacts with the customer has no more clue as to what to do differently, than they did before the training class.

And the problem is not just the use of buzz words or phrases. A detailed explanation of the complex inter-relationship between a customer's satisfaction and the service provider who must deliver it, without any idea of 'how' to actually do it, can still sound mesmerizingly impressive. For example, take this well intended customer service advice:

"Optimal results are only obtained when organizations take a holistic view of all customer channels and manage voice of the customer initiatives as part of a comprehensive program. These programs deliver considerable benefits, when the efforts are data driven with clear goals and expectations. It complements and extends traditional CRM by capturing customer requirements and feedback in order to provide best in class products and services. This type of process is proactive and constantly innovative in an attempt to capture the changing requirements of customers over time."[15]

What??? Jargon alert. Whenever some astute customer satisfaction visionary says something like this to you, challenge them and be ready with your own questions. Start out by asking them specifically 'how' what they are suggesting can be used by the employees that work with your customers. If they can't explain it in a way that allows you to implement it within your organization so that everyone knows what they now need to do, just thank them and walk away.

"People use jargon because they want to sound smart and credible when in fact they sound profoundly dim-witted and typically can't be understood, which defeats the purpose of speaking in the first place," says Karen Friedman, author of *Shut Up and Say Something*.[16]

The best customer service training tool will be one that can be used in any situation, with any customer, at any time, and give some feedback as to its appropriateness to that specific and unique situation the customer is currently in. Make sense? Then, stay tuned.

Why is Customer Satisfaction Difficult to Define?

Why do you think organizations have a hard time summing up what they want done in terms of customer service, and why is understanding the customer so difficult?

Well, for starters, customers are people and they're potentially all different... all 7 billion of them. Besides, often you can get different reactions from the same person to the same situation at different times. And different people will react differently to the same situation. Further, the optimum solution is usually case by case, and customized to the individual and the unique circumstances at that moment in time. This customized service delivery complicates successful execution, making it more difficult to 'standardize' service delivery or to rely on consistent policy pronouncements. That's why some companies oftentimes give some vague end-result guidance, and leave it up to the employee standing in front of the customer to use their own judgment to come up with the best customer solution. While it's an easy way out, different employees will have different responses, sometimes adjusted due to the situation and the emotions of the moment, which makes it difficult to have consistently excellent customer outcomes.

The idea that the solution to defining customer satisfaction will involve this 'individualization' of service delivery is suggested in a recent advertisement from Starwood® Hotels, generally viewed as one of the forward-looking companies when it comes to the customer. They said that their service delivery goal was 'for every visitor, a unique experience.'[17] But even in this case, shouldn't it be a unique 'good' experience, and what does that really mean anyway?

While it may be challenging, understanding the concept of customer satisfaction can lead to some very specific outcomes, which every successful organization should have as part of their goals. These positive customer outcomes, described in a 2017 article entitled, "5 Companies with Envy-Worthy Customer Experience," suggested that these companies were able to: Manage feedback effectively and wow customers consistently, resulting in higher customer satisfaction and loyalty, lower churn, increased revenue, and better overall business results.[18]

 With achieving these goals in mind, we'll move on to attempting to define customer Satisfaction.

Defining Customer Satisfaction

Like any good story, there are usually two sides: Organizations that provide customer service and the customer. And they often look at their interactions from two different perspectives.

Customer Satisfaction from a Service Provider's Viewpoint:
Just like a manufacturing company decides how to produce their product from their point of view, customer service is an internal self-defined concept. The organization creating the product or providing the service usually defines it as a series of attributes the organization feels their customers are looking for them to provide. Then, they ask their customers to grade the organization's pre-defined customer service attributes, to try to determine the level of customer satisfaction they provide.

Each company can define customer satisfaction its own way. It can also establish the level of service that they feel should be acceptable to their customers. Take complaint resolution for example. Each business develops company policies and guidelines that basically provides limits on the authority their service recovery employees have and need to follow, when trying to resolve customer issues. Managers know that some customers can be unreasonable in their demands, and so they want controls in place so employees don't 'give away the store' in an attempt to satisfy a customer.

So, defining general customer service guidelines usually consists of an internal self-assessment of the service they are willing/capable of providing, often irrespective of how their competition defines it or even what their customers expect. Then, they look for attributes to break-down and attempt to quantify the customer's satisfaction received, from the product or service they provide. These usually include speed of service (although sometimes a less rushed more relaxed and interactive response is what the customer wants). Other attributes might include the attitude and appearance of the service provider, the greeting, the ambience, the environment (hot/cold, look/feel, noise level, clean, safe, ease of doing business with the company, etc.).

From this internal assessment, company standards are developed. These standards, good or bad, end up defining the customer service culture within which the employees operate. It's from this, whether intended by management or not, that employees learn about the limits of their authority and the importance the company places on satisfying the customer.

When companies learn (the easy way or the hard way) that the customer is actually in charge of their company's future success, sometimes they change. Because in reality, providing quality customer service is more than just compliance to self-defined standards. But as a starting point, looking at a company's 'service standards' does give some insight into why some companies do a better job at customer satisfaction than others. We'll explore measuring these attributes that contribute to customer satisfaction in the next chapter.

Customer Satisfaction from a Customer's Viewpoint: If every customer represents a potentially unique set of needs and wants, it should be clear that if you want every customer to be satisfied, you can't treat every customer the same. And saying things like, "we need to provide excellent service to every guest, every time," is not only meaningless, it's unhelpful to those that are responsible for customer service delivery. Yet writing specific customer service guidelines that attempt to train employees to deliver customized/personalized customer service to every individual on the planet is clearly impossible.

So, to help simplify things like customer service delivery, companies group their customers, and the products and services they provide, into categories. Take restaurants for example. Those that serve customers looking for quick service and low prices, are 'fast-food.' Other restaurants are labeled 'fine dining' with the rest falling into every discrete grouping between. Communicating the service level helps set customer expectations and maximize a company's ability to predict and deliver the anticipated customer service level. But making the customer 'fit' into the company's pre-determined expectation model is sometimes challenging.

In the hospitality industry, hotels call themselves convention hotels or business hotels or leisure/resort hotels (or extended-stay or focused-service, etc.), in an attempt to simplify the challenge of setting (or more precisely, limiting) customer expectations.

This may make sense, until you realize the fact that your customer can be part of one market segment one day and another one the next. Guests can also be looking for multiple categories of service levels all at once, or sometimes none of the categories fit.

Ultimately, if you take maximizing customer experience to its logical conclusion, you come back to the realization that every customer interaction is potentially unique. And if you consider the enormity of the situation, in terms of how to train/equip employees with the tools necessary to satisfy an infinite number of wants and needs, organizations default back to meaningless vague pronouncements like: 'treat every customer with courtesy and respect,' leaving the nebulous goal of customized customer satisfaction delivery up to the individual employee.

So, what is customer satisfaction from the customer's perspective? It's the product and/or service level that an individual customer wants/expects, at that specific location, and at that specific time, compared to their perception (whether real or imagined) of the service level experienced. The customer service employee soon faces the fact that customers possess an unlimited uniqueness of perspectives and an infinite combination of situations and customer experiences that they must deal with.[19]

So how do they deal with it? The reality is that if employees are not trained and not given the right tools to satisfy a broad range of customer situations, they defensively become better at coping then seeking out a solution. And often, policies and procedures limit the range of choices that an employee has available to resolve an issue or complaint. So, if the solution is outside the limits of the employee's authority, the employee finds ways to detach. For example, they may apologize and 'take the heat' of a customer's dissatisfaction, trying to remain un-phased at the customer's threats of lost future business. So, what can you do to help the employee not just cope, but have a customer interchange that leads to a higher customer satisfaction outcome?

First, when giving guidance and trying to positively influence employees in their training sessions, don't focus on the outcome, focus on behavior. Setting goals and objectives are important components of leadership. The mistake most people make is they focus on outcomes rather than the behaviors needed to change to accomplish the outcome.

Managers need to do the hard work of actually deciding and providing guidance to employees about not only what needs to be done but also 'how' to do it, in order to actually accomplish the goals and objectives they've established. So, avoid telling people just what to achieve. Instead, coach them on what to do given the situation, and then explain how to do it.

Chapter Summary
The concept of customer satisfaction 'in as many ways as possible' is vague and not actionable. But in a way, it does describe the real situation that faces anyone trying to provide customer satisfaction. It really comes down to potentially satisfying every person on the planet, every time, even though they may have different wants and needs, at different times and places, and may not even express them to you, or even know what they are. Maybe that's why, even those who are successful at it, find it difficult to define.

Ultimately, the solution is that the customer service employee needs to discover what the customer expectations are, and develop a talent for delivering customized/individualized customer satisfaction, by exceeding those expectations.

The solution? Develop the behavior talent of 'how' to deliver individualized customer satisfaction, as that is the key to sustained customer loyalty. Giving you the specific, actionable tools to accomplish this, is the goal of this book.

Chapter 2: Measuring Customer Satisfaction

Now that we've considered the challenges of defining customer satisfaction, how is it measured?

Most companies understand that customer service levels determine future operational success, and should therefore be measured, managed and improved. The problem is that while financials lend themselves to numerical results (dollars, units, time) and are therefore quantifiable and relatively easy to measure, customer service levels (feelings, emotions, attitudes, and expectations), do not. Whether it's in person, on the phone, using mail/email, through social media, web sites or 3rd party apps, companies spend millions trying to measure the level of customer service/customer satisfaction they are providing. So, what are some of the challenges when trying to measure customer feedback?

As discussed in the previous chapter, with so many variables affecting service delivery, combined with unique service expectations and the uncertainty of human nature itself, just defining customer satisfaction is the first challenge. As a result, when facing the issue of actually measuring customer satisfaction, most service providers just come up with a set or collection of service attributes they currently provide. Then they try to find out how well they are delivering those attributes, by asking the customer to rate them. The first issue is that while organizations may know what they provide, they may be oblivious to what their customer expects. For example, you should all know what set of attributes represent the essence of your organization or brand, but what if it's different from what your customers expect? Therefore, significant research into what *your* current or future customers expect, needs to be done before even asking them to rate their experience.

Obviously knowing something is better than nothing, so despite these limitations, any customer intelligence will give some insight into where improvement is needed. But because of the uniqueness of the individual customer's wants and needs, it's hard to train your customer service staff in anything other than customer service generalities.

Presumably, if the customer service questions you ask are not based on your customer's expectations, they will rate the attributes that are included lower, distorting the results. And worse, the customer may conclude after completing your survey that what they need is not what you provide. Hopefully, however, they will use the free form 'suggestions/other comments' section to describe the service areas omitted. Use these remarks to improve the accuracy of your process.

But also attempt to get some external market research and competitive data, so you can develop new products or services, or extensions of what you already provide to expand your customer base and reach new customers. Therefore, while you should keep a core base of basic questions that allow for period-to-period comparisons over time, the questions you ask to measure customer expectations and the research that follows should be constantly evolving. Then, use the customer feedback as part of your ongoing customer intelligence knowledge base, using it to modify and enhance the products and services you provide.

Numerical responses to questions help tabulate and analyze data, but customer comments that offer specific feedback tend to be more useful and actionable. Some companies are using text recognition applications that search free-form comments for key words, and then group comments into relevant subject areas. And forward-looking companies like Hyatt Hotels are working to integrate customer's individual answers into its guest profiles, so more targeted products and services can be delivered on subsequent visits. As Hyatt explains, "We need to balance customer privacy in the information they share, with letting them know we are listening to them and want to personalize their stay."[20]

Traditional Measurements of Customer Satisfaction

It doesn't matter if it's J. D. Power and Associates®, the American Customer Satisfaction Institute®, Consumer Reports® or you do it yourself, measurement of customer satisfaction levels usually starts with some type of formalized questions listed in an interview/survey format, presented in person, by phone, mail, email, web or smart device application. It consists of a series of customer attributes set against a letter, word, symbol, star, diamond, emoji, or numerical scale.

While this has the advantage of being able to quantify the customer experience score the company received, if the company doesn't know who delivered the experience, it may not be corrected if it was bad, or rewarded if it was good.

And while it gives some insight into the level of customer satisfaction, the rating itself isn't helpful in determining what else could have been done to raise the score. In addition, you may also be asking the wrong questions or measuring the wrong attributes. That's where allowing for free-form verbatim text comments helps to clarify the rationale behind the grades the customer gives. We also earlier discussed the concept of expectations, and the fact that providing the same service level to everyone can yield different ratings due to each individual customer having potentially a unique set of expectations.

Ultimately, the measurement of a customer's satisfaction level, represents that particular customer's opinion of the service received for a particular customer service attribute or group of attributes, subtracted from the expectations the customer thought they would receive. As a result, expectations can be exceeded, met, or not met, and this is usually the criteria the customer uses when deciding how to rate any given attribute, including their overall experience.

Evaluating the customer service received is helpful, but knowing if you provided value adds an additional dimension. So, when price paid is overlaid against the service received, customer opinions can change. As a general rule, however, the higher the price paid, the higher the expectations and the lower the price paid including zero, the lower the expectations. As a result, the same service level may seem to be good at some lower price, but not at some higher one. However, even when something is provided for free, there is still some expectation that the product will perform at some minimum level, and if it's a service, that it will exceed some minimum acceptable expectation level. The concept of 'value received' is complex and how the questions are asked and how the data is evaluated can create misleading impressions if these multiple inter-related factors are not properly taken into consideration. About the best we can conclude in this general discussion is that the higher your product/service standards exceed your current/future customer expectations and the higher you are able to deliver against those standards, the higher the price you can receive, and still provide value.

If customers of a business are asked for their feedback, the broader the sample of randomly chosen respondents, the more representative, and valid the feedback. Working against this is the fact that some customers make it a point to regularly provide formal feedback (fill out surveys, respond to calls, emails and other requests seeking feedback), while others never do. That's why it's important to also have some type of informal feedback process. It may be just the unobtrusive insertion of an informal verbal question during a routine customer interaction that gets tallied, or nearby staff members that serve as listening posts who obtain informal customer feedback indirectly. If you're able to capture and accumulate feedback from those who generally do not respond to formal requests, it gives you an advantage. At minimum, it can be used to validate results from formal feedback. And, if in real time, it has the additional advantage of allowing for a recognition component if positive, or instituting your service recovery process right away, if something goes wrong.

'After the Fact' Feedback

The old adage, 'you can't manage what you can't measure,'[21] is true in customer satisfaction situations as well. Usually, when people talk about customer satisfaction 'measurement' they generally mean an assessment of satisfaction from the customer. Then companies use it to compare the score to prior periods made up of mostly other customers, or to competitive company or industry averages to benchmark how they are doing. The problem is that this is all after the fact. The customer interaction has occurred and has concluded, and 'it is what it is', and negative impressions have been made and may remain. So, feedback after the customer has concluded the transaction, limits the service recovery options.

No matter how accurate, the lack of quantifiable measures in real time, works against both the employee and the organization. The employee wants to do the right thing, but without tools to gauge the service level they are providing at any given moment, much less the satisfaction level being received from the customer's perspective, they tend to take the path of least resistance, and just apologize for missteps that occurred in the past, and offer a promise about the future.

Offsets and Averages

At the individual survey questionnaire level, some of the questions being asked represent attributes that can either offset or support each other. Sometimes, a customer satisfaction question will attempt to cover general conditions like cleanliness, physical condition, or even staff courtesy (we'll define these later as 'foundational' attributes). They are used to get to the customer's overall impression of the product/service being provided. While this offers the advantage of obtaining the general impression of the attribute, the disadvantages are, it's not specific, may be offset by other similar factors, and if correction is needed, it may not be specific enough to be actionable. For example, take cleanliness. Some areas may be clean and some not. The clean area should get an 'A' rating and the unclean area an 'F'. The typical customer asked to rate cleanliness overall, might tend to give an average grade of 'C'. In addition, companies can define customer service levels differently, and customers can interpret them differently as well. In any given situation, the service provider may think they delivered the service well and the customer may not feel the same way. Was the customer's expectation unreasonably high or was the company's service standards set too low?

What's wrong with having your employees just ask the customer their level of satisfaction? Well, for starters, customers being asked to rate the employee standing in front of them, may give inflated grades, in order to avoid any confrontation. (How was everything? Oh, everything was fine). And, a customer who has decided not to make any future investments in your business may not see the value of even sharing their time and effort in providing you with feedback. Besides, how do you quantify the customer's tone of voice, or a facial expression or even hidden intention or anger after you've told the customer 'no'? And, what about something good, delivered with a bad attitude?

While it's not uncommon for an employee to ask you if everything is all right, the customer's response is generally not a good indication of the level of service they feel they've been provided. Also consider that while asking the customer if their expectations were met may seem reasonable at first, individual reactions to the same service delivery level may be different. And as we've mentioned, even the same customer may react differently at different times, even if the service level was the same.

Despite the disadvantages, the post-experience survey is still the most common way of obtaining customer feedback (although as we'll discuss later, this may be changing). Therefore, for both individual companies themselves and for the multi-billion-dollar third party customer research industry, post-experience customer data gathering is still the norm. For the customer, it generally takes the form of answering a series of pre-determined questions, with usually a free-form open-ended question at the end. Comment forms/cards, telephone prompted surveys or web-based questionnaires to answer post-experience, are some of the standard methods. And mobile device attachments, email links and geotag pop-up surveys, among others, are some of the other methods companies use to get these questionnaires in front of their customers. In addition, most websites that support on-line chat inquiries and customer-initiated calls to service centers now include an opt-in, post-call satisfaction survey. And retailers, from fast food to grocery stores are including 'chances to win incentives' on their post-shopping receipt, all in an attempt to generate customer feedback. This leads us to the issue of reliability.

Reliability

Reporting of statistical survey results are problematic to start with. Statistics are by definition subject to interpretation. They've been manipulated, distorted, and used to justify biased positions probably from the beginning of time and certainly before, "How to Lie with Statistics," by Darrell Huff,[22] became a best seller back in 1954. (He famously reminded us that "correlation does not imply causation").

Gathering accurate information is also difficult. Getting a relevant population sample to respond to surveys is a challenge in itself. As mentioned, there are those that may have relevant input, but never respond, and responses from fringe 'manic responders,' may not be representative.

And just like the reliability of the feedback is questionable if the asker is standing in front of you, written comments can yield unreliable results as well. When a respondent does decide to complete a survey, they may be untruthful or inaccurate or both. (Incentives, bonuses and rewards for responding may exacerbate the problem).

But in general, all survey respondents generally work through 4 steps:
1. Interpret the meaning of a question
2. Recall all relevant facts/experiences related to the question
3. Internally summarize those facts/compare them to the question
4. Summarize their judgment and respond accurately

Factors affecting the reliability of feedback when going through the mental processes to complete a questionnaire include:

- Attitude: That can range from boredom and disinterest to deliberate distortion of responses. (Unsolicited feedback, like web-based evaluations have shown to be even more exaggerated, tending to the extremes).
- Circumstances: Respondents may also be rushed, multi-tasking, distracted, or might just respond in any fashion, (including checking all 1s or all 10s), just to get the survey over with. There may also be situations where early questions are given more attention than later ones, or the first logical choice is made without reviewing the other options that follow.

As a result, respondents often take shortcuts, which researchers in this space have described as 'satisficing,' a term that is a blend of satisfy and suffice. According to the laws of economics, consumers are supposed to select the optimal product or service that maximizes *utility*[23] received i.e., meets/exceeds their needs for price (including time/effort) paid. But in reality, consumers often choose a satisfactory solution rather than the optimal solution, because it is too time consuming to evaluate all the available alternatives.

Likewise, when customers complete surveys, respondents are supposed to select the optimal answer, but respondents often choose just a satisfactory answer instead. Using the four mental steps above, when a respondent works through each step with a maximum level of effort, they are optimizing their answers. When they skip the steps of recall and internal summarization (Steps 2 & 3) and still answer the question, they are 'strongly satisficing' or 'cheating.'[24]

Letting the respondent know in the introduction the importance of providing accurate answers (like improved service for them in the future) may or may not improve reliability. One technique, used to improve reliability is to selectively, after some questions, ask the respondent to clarify/justify their previous answer with an open-ended question. Another approach, is to ask a question, and later in the questionnaire, ask for disagreement with the opposite of the same question, to test respondent's response reliability. Randomization of who completes the surveys helps make the results more statistically valid, as does anonymity, but prevents follow-up service recovery.

Also, don't measure for the sake of measuring. I've met with executives who, when asked why they chose a particular data set to analyze and use to make business decisions, have told me, because we have the data 'right here'.

Finally, keep it simple.   Make sure relevant customer intelligence gathered isn't obscured by too much information. And, use the results. Always look for ways to make internal recommendations for improvement, derived from the analysis of data, actionable.

How the question is worded is also important. Proper wording can mean the difference between getting insight into the customer's expectations, versus obtaining a bunch of useless (or wrong) feedback. For example, avoid the tendency to measure overall impressions that may represent a combination of customer considerations; e.g. on a scale of 1-10, were you happy with the service you received? Rather, measure the key indicators to evaluating your organization's performance and predict future success. i.e., what did you like best, and what else can we do to make your experience even better next time?

Impact of Technology on Customer Feedback

Internet and Email: The '00 decade introduced businesses to an accelerated pace of responsiveness with the increased use of on-line internet access. A quick response used to be defined in days. Now, in the second decade of the 21st century we've transitioned from quick response to real-time response. Advances in both wireless and smart device technology have been the impetus for this further evolution. Connections moved beyond desk top computing to smaller more portable devices, and not just for voice, but for data (including photos and videos) as well. Now, with millions of customers using mobile devices every day, companies are scrambling to utilize and exploit advanced wireless technology and the ever-increasing feature benefits of new applications for customer smart devices.

For example, hotels are looking to further increase their connection and speed of dialog with their customers. It started by developing their own 'bring your own device' (BYOD) strategies. Now, with everyone carrying their own smart devices, it's all about getting their 'app' on the customer's device. Also, working with hospitality tech companies, they are developing new services for guests, through their applications such as: selecting specific rooms at time of reservation, and with improved GPS location information, providing specific offers and benefits based on where you are. Also, using near field communications (NFC), and radio frequency identification (RFID) technology, smart devices can become an encrypted electronic 'key' that can be used to access your guest room, or other secured or value-added service areas.

The applications can also provide location-based or interest based in-stay hotel information as well as be used to pay (or dispute) your bill, eliminating the need to stop by the front desk, at the beginning, during or at the end of your stay. Other technologies, like Bluetooth beacons and enabled mobile devices will provide network security integrity, encryption of data, and biometric identification. And, as customers migrate from smart phones/tablets to wearable devices, opt-in tracking is going to be transformational in the way customers receive and send feedback information. Companies are trying to find out the best ways to gather, use, and respond to these new customer technology capabilities, just as old forms of communications (comment cards, phone surveys, and customer service hotlines) are disappearing.

They will have the capabilities to not only track your location so product/service delivery can be brought to you, but provide location specific information on nearby attractions, as well as instant communication for problem resolution to survey customer issues, and respond to them as they are happening.

Other examples? According to a recent article by Matt Brownell,[25] "…the contribution [that Google] Glass could make to customer service goes beyond just filming disputes: Customer service technology firm Genesys recently floated a couple of scenarios in a blog post. A customer trying to assemble a cable box, for instance, could beam his or her field of vision to technical support staff, who would then be able to see the problem and direct the customer on what to do next. They also suggest that a hotel guest out and about with Glass could send live video to a concierge, who could then identify what part of town he was in, and recommend restaurants and nearby attractions…"   And other technologies like Augmented Reality (AR) can show the customer engaged in the experience, like the view from a particular hotel room or stadium seat, in advance of the purchase.

Privacy concerns become more important, but can be mitigated by simple profile opt-in/out elections. And, while technology applications and web use continue to grow, never thought of features and functionality will be developed, as more and more travelers carry, or wear or one day, are imbedded with micro smart devices.

Impact of 'Social Media' on Customer Feedback

To product/service providers, this technology evolution has its advantages, as it increases the access and speed of response to their customers.   But it has also unleashed the customer's ability to communicate directly with other customers. Customers now have the ability to share reviews and comments on service levels for all of us to see, since those that provide products/service, no longer control the dialog.

Unsolicited Customer Feedback: Earlier, we talked about the value of formal, periodic surveying of customers to get the customer's feedback on how satisfied they were and what could be done to improve survey scores.   But things have changed.   Business executives feel that customers still share their comments with them.   But they have also mentioned that now, if a customer feels that we're not listening, or if they feel they don't have leverage and we're not going to help them, they are more likely to use other indirect outlets, like internet evaluation websites, to express their feelings.

With the explosion of social user-generated content (or simply 'social media') sites like *Twitter, Trip Advisor, Amazon reviews, Yelp*, etc., customers aren't using traditional company feedback and survey channels and they're not waiting to be asked their opinion. The voice of the customer (VOC), a well-worn phrase, is no longer the result of companies asking the questions and choosing the audience. Social media has empowered the customer and they have taken the control of what is said and who hears it, out of the hands of companies. Directionally, instead of companies 'pulling' information from the customers in a methodical and formatted way, social media customers are now 'pushing' their feedback to companies, customers, and the marketplace. And, with 3rd party websites now serving as an aggregator of unsolicited customer feedback, customers are empowered to share their comments, observations, opinions, and experiences, in their own way, and on their own terms.

But as customer feedback migrates from just product/service provider feedback survey solicitation, new issue and trends have appeared. We've mentioned that with unsolicited and unstructured customer feedback, those that chose to provide responses to these 3rd party sites tend to comment at extremes. And, results may be biased by high frequency responders, or by commenters that didn't use the product or service. So, despite the often-large numbers of respondents due to the easy access to feedback sites on the internet, the feedback still may not be representative.

Emotional responses are also encouraged by the ease with which customers can rant (and sometimes distort) their social network feedback. Similarly, those with just an average experience, or those without a story may not choose to respond, even though they may have valuable insights for improvement. Knowing what the 'middle' thinks and how the company could have done better for this important category of customers tends to be missing. And, as mentioned, offering incentives like discounts or chances at gift cards or free items may increase response rates, but at the same time may diminish/distort the value of the data by biased or forced feedback.

Perhaps more significantly, the intended recipient/audience isn't even the company in question; it's their fellow peers, and the company's potential future customers. The voice of the customer is now loud and getting louder, and they're not just telling you, they're telling the world. In fact, the customer now decides everything: what feedback is provided and how, as well as where and when it's given. And your prospective customers are not only listening to their fellow travelers, they're using the information to make purchase decisions. For example, in the hospitality industry, 72 percent of consumers claim they trust online reviews as much as personal recommendations, and an astonishing 35 percent of travelers have admitted to changing their hotel reservations after reading online reviews, from people they don't even know.[26]

So, it's clear that the customer feedback world has changed. With over 90% of online adults using a social networking site,[27] your customer doesn't need to talk to you; they are sharing their feedback directly with your potential customers. And, your current and future customers are listening, because what customers tell others is perceived as more relevant than what you are trying to say in your PR releases and advertisements.

Despite these issues, just the fact that a customer offers to communicate their view of their experience with your product or service, should make the customer focused company drop everything and listen. And if you're too busy to be listening, and rely on only internally generated feedback, you do so at your own peril.

Opportunities Created by Social Media: Leaders in customer responsiveness have tapped into this external resource and actively monitor social media sites, so they can get feedback that is otherwise unavailable to them through company generated traditional feedback mechanisms. It's more expensive for the company to gather, but it contains the current and the historical comments on products/services they provide and gives the company an opportunity to proactively respond as necessary. In fact, since the customer is providing feedback to other potential customers, there's an expectation that the company isn't even aware of their feedback. After all, if they wanted just the company to receive it, they would have sent it to them directly.

But this has led to opportunity. There are some interesting examples of customer's being 'wowed' by creative companies that monitor customer comments on social media, and immediately address the issue in a creative way. For example, a local business that monitors Yelp.com learns of a customer concern about their product or service and replies to the concern on Yelp.com offering them a refund, an upgrade, and a cost-free replacement as well as an apology. Or, a honeymoon couple tweets about their disappointment, that while checking-in at the Pineapple Resort, a room with an ocean view was not available but that they were going to make the best of it for the next three nights. How amazing would it be if the Pineapple Resort was monitoring posts about them and could respond to that honeymoon couple with champagne and strawberries tonight and an offer of an upgrade to an ocean view suite tomorrow?

You can also use the legacy systems and information you already have, to create your own social media 'buzz.' For example, an airline having date of birth information in opt-in customer profiles, can deliver flowers or a small birthday gift at the airport (or when first seated) before takeoff, as a result of internally coordinated data alerts, catching the customer totally off guard (in the delight/surprise/wow! realm), while those around applaud, as the airline watches existing customer loyalty soar. And, when the story is retold, and potentially goes 'viral,' it generates positive feedback to other potential customers in a way unavailable without social media.

How well companies utilize social media (monitoring/anticipating and responding immediately in real time) will be the new battleground for customer satisfaction. Major global brands at the macro level as well as operating units at the micro level are taking notice.

Companies that will lead in customer loyalty in the future will leverage social media, which, if handled correctly, will not only improve the emotional engagement the customer feels with the company, but can benefit the customer in terms of more timely service and issue/problem resolution. It will also tend to force the hand of those under-performing/ complaint prone companies, to improve.

Before social media, the old adage was, a happy customer tells 2 people, and a dissatisfied customer tells 10. Now, happy customers tell a hundred, and dissatisfied customers tell a million. Not only has the power and control of customer feedback and data shifted from the seller to the buyer, but the impact and importance of Social Media has dramatically increased as well.[28]

Social media also has the potential to weaken so called 'branding power' as the exclusive realm of setting customer expectations. It has spawned new opportunities for companies to distinguish themselves from the competition in the eyes of their customers, through the collection and use of the social media comments readily available to them. Some proactive unit managers are seeking out social media comments and taking the initiative to respond within the context of the original comment for all to see. Sometimes it's an apology and a note to contact them directly so the company can 'make it right' with the customer. Sometimes it's a thank you for a positive comment. It's a growing tool to engage in a two-way dialog with your customer, to learn what they expect now and, in the future, while providing others with a glimpse of your service culture.

One note of caution. If you plan to monitor customer complaints and input through social media, remember it's a public forum. For example, if you offer a refund for reportedly less than perfect service, just be prepared to do it consistently, as it becomes a global expectation and can become a negative if not done for everyone in a similar situation. And, it may also inadvertently encourage exaggerated dissatisfaction claims. Usually, it's best to apologize and ask the complaining customer to contact you directly. Then, offer a service recovery solution off-line.

Capturing Real-Time Feedback

Pre/During/Post Purchase: Usually, the longer the time lapse between the problem and its resolution, the higher the cost, both in expense of resolution and risk of customer loss. Companies have recognized that the quicker they can respond to a customer problem, the easier (and cheaper) it is to resolve the complaint. They also realize that real time feedback allows for real time customer solutions. (You'll find the 'Give Yourself A Number' method is ideally suited for the new trend of real-time customer satisfaction/service recovery, when the GYAN process is introduced in Chapter 7). More timely feedback also empowers the employee to make corrections based on immediate customer feedback. It can also facilitate the ongoing two-way real-time link between customers and service providers during the current transaction, as well as in subsequent transactions.

Organizations know that they will enjoy more customer loyalty if they can prevent customer complaints, or at least correct them as soon as they occur. But how can a service provider know the moment something becomes an issue for the customer?

An important tenet of Marketing 101 is to maintain an ongoing commitment and engagement with your customer base. But today, that could become a 24/7/365 possibility, as companies strive to find the right balance: stay in touch through real-time communications and incentives while not overloading the customer with marketing information, and constant requests for feedback. Suheel Sheikh, branch manager for Chase Bank in California, concluded that, "Real time feedback seems to be the obvious challenge to most businesses as they do want to know how they're doing, it's the most pertinent time to deliver the best experience possible, yet it's the most difficult time to solicit/survey clients without sounding intrusive."[29]

In the past, most companies chose the post-purchase questionnaire/ survey as their primary means for gathering customer feedback. Now, forward looking companies are expanding their feedback window so that the actual customer feedback process would start from initial contact pre-purchase, continue through the sales process, to product/service delivery and then finally end-user data on durability, and suitability of use, data on repair, replacement or refund, and subsequent purchases.

For example, in purchasing a product, like an appliance, the product provider would attempt to obtain customer feedback during the initial contact, and if the process continues, the feedback process would continue through the sales process, purchase, and post-purchase satisfaction measurement. Recently introduced smart appliances can monitor functionality continuously, and report its status, so that even minor preventative or performance issues can be addressed, before they become more expensive repairs. If it's a service, technology and the ease of social media applications can be used to facilitate this on-going feedback. For hotels, this would mean progressing from responding to problems reported post-stay, to actively and continuously monitoring the entire guest experience, beginning at time of reservations (pre-stay), then continuing with the arrival/check-in and throughout the hotel stay (in-stay) through the departure and ongoing readiness to accommodate future stay requests (post-stay).

The goal is to develop a continuous, unobtrusive two-way feedback loop, that keeps the customer and the product/service provider engaged, in real-time. Then, make it easy for a customer to provide feedback, like using a smart device app to report an issue or just make a request, since an immediate response and resolution has the potential to increase customer loyalty.

Hotel corporate websites and social media feedback websites like *Trip Advisor and Yelp* not only allow customers to communicate their experiences about your hotel, but also allow you to read the feedback from customers for competing hotels. Now, hotel companies have started to provide links between their websites and 3rd party social media sites.[30] Hotels typically don't broadcast negative comments from their guests, but social media has changed all that, showcasing the hotel's product/service weaknesses alongside their own biased advertisements. This added transparency allows prospective customers to see public reviews, showing businesses in all their glory, and with all their faults. This not only helps prospective customers, but provides an incentive to the service provider, to improve their service offering as well.

Managers of units that are part of a multi-unit network can no longer hide their customer problems and resolutions from regional or corporate management, and this in and of itself will tend to improve overall customer satisfaction. And, take the case of large franchise chains with the majority of their units not corporately managed. They rely on 3rd party owners/managers to properly represent and protect their brand (like *Best Western, McDonalds, Subway* sandwich shops, etc.). Social media helps, by putting added pressure on their franchisees and operators to improve or be removed from the system, all ultimately strengthening the brands while improving the future customer experience.

What about 'Outsourcing' Customer Research?

We've discussed how technology and social media developments have made it easier for customers to share their comments and for companies to gather their feedback, (and to see how the competition is performing). This information gathering can be handled directly between you and your customers, without the help of big customer research conglomerates that were traditionally relied upon to tell us what our customers were thinking. Now, any company can do the research themselves. The big customer research firms however hope you won't.

Feeling challenged, some world-wide customer research companies are already crowding the web with cautionary warnings, and touting the distortions and disadvantages of the 'Do It Yourself' (DIY) approach to customer research. They say it contains too much biased feedback, and there is too much sentiment/emotion in the comments.

And, a research paper[31] tries to frighten you by citing conflicting quotes within the same scalability topic heading. "The data is just too broad to be applicable to your specific brand/ product/situation." Then later stating: "The data is too specific and doesn't allow us to see the big picture without becoming uselessly obtuse."

Therefore, the message is, that you need these big customer research companies to help interpret what's out there. Their approach? Use big, scary words: "However, scaling and targeting the massive amounts of data to fit the objectives of the research is the penultimate benefit of human research and annotation." They go on to talk about "...complex query development and data synthesis, 'Computational Linguistics', and the 'Complex Boolean logic' methodology they use." No surprise that they conclude with the statement, "Therefore, it's important to employ research experts..."

On the other hand, while access to customer data is readily available, if you don't have the internal resources, research firms can provide valuable assistance with not only obtaining the data, but in managing, analyzing and summarizing large amounts of customer and competitive data, into meaningful customer intelligence.

There are many well respected organizations that are experts at gathering customer satisfaction data. Customer research and customer feedback acquisition is a multi-billion-dollar global industry. You need to decide if outsourcing the customer feedback process is right for you, and if you do, which group can deliver the most value. Make sure their capabilities meet your needs. Verify that the customer feedback provider you are considering can collect information from all the channels your customers use, and verify that they have the analytical capabilities to make the information not only relevant, but useful.

Also, make sure that you both have a shared common vision and that they look at the customer experience the same way that you do. Verify that their systems integrate with yours and that they are not just collecting data, but providing actionable information to corporate staff and the operating units as well. They may have a competence in the information gathering process; attribute selection, comparative industry trends, etc., that internally, your company may not have. They can also free-up valuable internal resources for other value related activities.

Take the following sentence, which could have been written to promote the services of any of the 'big house' customer experience measurement companies: "We'll show you how to measure and what to measure to drive improvement and innovation in customer experience management." Sounds nice, but just make sure you keep a 'clarity' perspective. Setting targets, and knowing the current level of the customer satisfaction your product or service is delivering is important. It will uncover the 'what' as in what is my current situation, what do I do well, what do I need to improve, etc. 'How,' will you use the information to improve is a completely separate issue, and one that's more challenging for the 'data warehousing people' to help you with.

Foundational and Experiential Dimensions

Separating the Foundational (how it works) and the Experiential attributes (how it feels) creates information that allows the product/service provider to create actionable responses/solutions throughout the customer experience.

A pre-purchase, purchase/use, and post-use feedback model can ideally give you a continuous view of the level of customer satisfaction you are providing. And, looking at these three stages of your interaction with the customer, based on the two dimensions of foundational and experiential value you provide your customers, allows forward looking companies to get a more complete picture of the customer's view on the product/service they receive. This ongoing dialogue allows you to make those inevitable 'mid-course' corrections. We'll cover this in more detail in Part II, when we discuss Customer Loyalty, but for now, a focus on getting this more complete customer perspective, will allow you to better predict repeat business and loyalty/advocacy.

And finally, as to feedback timing, the reality is that today's customers can provide real time feedback on your product or service whether or not you ask for it. They are in continuous contact with friends/ acquaintances, and with millions of your current or potential future customers through social media and the web. Your only real decision to make, is if you wish to capture (and use) it or not.

What's the solution to getting timely, relevant and actionable customer feedback, and linking it to the concepts we've learned, based on your business model and the customers you serve?

A 'full spectrum' approach, that includes the 'time-linear' component: pre-purchase/purchase/and post-purchase, evaluated based on the 'foundational' and 'experiential' dimensions that your product and service provides, that would provide feedback developed internally as well as externally.

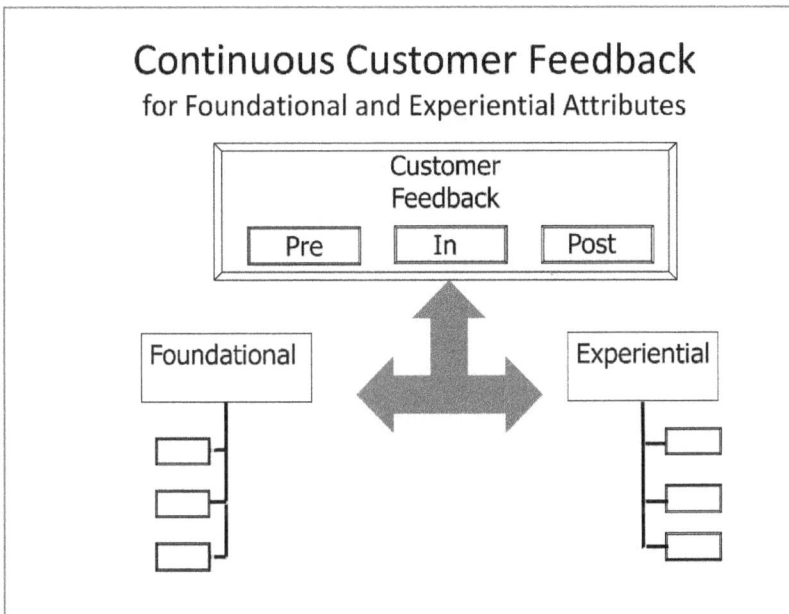

Figure 2-1: Continuous Customer Feedback

Chapter Summary
It's not hard to envision a time when a customer's mobile device provides the platform for instant customer feedback on services you provide. As for products, it will be the product itself providing the feedback, as smart appliances, passively informs your service group of maintenance they may need, all in real time.

Advancing technology and a social media culture is forever changing the way we measure how satisfied our customers are with our products and services. Companies are no longer limited to analyzing post-transaction feedback, as technology offers the promise of real-time feedback over the full timeline of the customer experience.

In addition to technological advances impacting feedback, social media has turned the tables on the entire process of customer feedback and measurement. Formal surveys designed and distributed by companies had been the norm, and problems/complaints and their resolution were usually kept between the company and the affected customer. Social media changed all that. Customers can quickly share their rant with thousands of interested individuals and future potential customers. And something that is starting to register with customer service focused companies, is that the feedback from their customer's peers is often being weighted more heavily and is having more influence on future customers' purchase decisions, than company generated, promotions, pronouncements and advertisements.

But don't worry. The focus you have on improving customer satisfaction is still correct. The stakes are now just higher. Your customer's impressions can create advocacy as satisfied customers end up joining, and becoming a credible extension of your marketing effort ...or don't.

Chapter 3: Delivering Customer Satisfaction

The Customer Service Employee

Ironically, in a typical service business, the more experience an employee has in a customer facing job, the more isolated they are from direct customer interaction. The newest of the new are usually pushed to center stage with the customer, as they try to figure out on their own, what to do with the customer in front of them. Despite the fact that customer satisfaction is so complex, the supervisor with all the experience ends up, not only not in front of the customer, but begins to enjoy their isolation from them. This may not be the situation in your organization, but in some companies, customer contact positions are usually viewed as a prerequisite to advancement… an entry level position where you 'pay your dues.' And like other 'dirty jobs' where you have to survive to get promoted, you don't want to go through it again. Besides, you're now a 'boss' and you have important administrative things to do, things much more important than dealing with customers.

Then there's dealing with customer complaints. It's also usually the newest, least experienced employee with the least authority that a complaining customer first meets.

A classic customer complaint scenario goes like this:

Customer: I have a complaint about my bill.
Employee: I don't have the authority to adjust your bill.
Customer: Who does have the authority?
Employee: My manager.
Customer: May I speak to your manager.
Employee: S/he's not available.

It's a situation that gets repeated over and over again a million times a day. An upset customer may put your financial future at risk directionally, but at the moment, there is nothing in the untrained employee's playbook that will help keep the customer's business.

One of the solutions would be, if you could instill in every employee the owner's perspective. Some of the best restaurant experiences I've had, occurred in small businesses where the owner is at the door seating guests. Their welcoming attitude and genuine concern for the customer spreads throughout the staff. They see she cares, so they care. The loyal customer following can be quite remarkable, as the business sometimes passes on from generation to generation. But in the real world in general, customer contact employees don't have the owner's perspective. Often underpaid and understaffed, caring employees will often default to doing the best they can, given the circumstances, and it may not be enough. But if employees are taught and understand the components of customer satisfaction, and are empowered and given the tools (like the GYAN process), they'll be in a better position to satisfy the customer.

Defining the Components of Customer Satisfaction

Those of us who operate in the realm of customer service (that's all of us) have a very interesting and challenging job. Thinking beyond just 'satisfying' the customer is what makes customer service interesting to me. Reciting the company policy manual verbiage is what makes customer service boring. We've said that each customer is potentially unique, and that's challenging enough, but add to that, customers don't always say what they want, or know what they want, and you start seeing the interesting part. If customer service was a 'one size fits all' it would be an easy job to train and an easy job to do. For example, if every customer likes and dislikes the same thing, and you know what it is, just give it to them. That's not the reality, and we should be thankful. Not just because satisfying a customer is a unique and interesting challenge, but with a little thought and insight, it gives your business an opportunity to go beyond just customer satisfaction, and deliver true customer loyalty.

In order to get a better understanding of what customer satisfaction is, it's helpful to review the different levels or degrees of customer satisfaction so we recognize the differences, determine what level we want to achieve, and then focus our training resources and our staff on delivering the desired customer outcomes.

The 5 Levels of Customer Satisfaction

Definitionally, satisfying customers involves delivering a product or service level that addresses their expected wants and needs. In my experience there is a hierarchy of five levels of customer satisfaction:

1. Unsatisfied or dissatisfied, or met some but not all needs
2. Satisfied-met expressed needs
3. Exceed expressed customer needs
4. Anticipate/satisfy un-expressed needs
5. Anticipate and exceed unexpressed and even unimagined needs (The realm of Delight, Surprise, and Wow!)

A visual representation might look like the following graphic:

Figure 3-1: Description of Five Levels of Customer Satisfaction

<u>Level 1: Not Satisfying the Customer:</u> Customers are important to every organization, and everyone says they want happy, satisfied customers. The reality is that not all customers are satisfied all the time. Sometimes you can explain it as they were too demanding, or what they were asking for was not available, or too expensive, or too unreasonable. Those that operate at Level 1 accept a certain number of dissatisfied customers.

They accept and consider it as part of the human condition, or part of the business they're in or the products they sell. The causes and the rationalizations are complex and varied, but no matter what your organization does, it won't be successful if you consistently operate it in Level 1.

Level 2: Satisfying the Customer: Most companies and most employees at Level 2, look at customer satisfaction as a 'did we or didn't we' satisfy the customer's needs. As mentioned, at some fundamental level, all companies want to satisfy customers. Sometimes they do, sometimes they don't, and are usually happy if they satisfy most. Basically, they are satisfied, when the customer is satisfied. Their 'target' is to hit the center of the bull's-eye of customer satisfaction… then they stop.

So, if Level 1 is not satisfying a customer, which not many companies have as a goal, satisfying a customer puts you at Level 2: the level of customer service at which all customer requests (customer expressed needs) that have been made, have been met. Companies that operate at Level 2 want to satisfy all their customers all the time. (But in the next chapter, we'll make the case that satisfying a customer isn't enough to ensure repeat purchases, advocacy, or customer loyalty).

Level 3: Exceeding Customer Expectations: Some people are unaware that there is even a next level beyond a satisfied customer. They focus on satisfied or unsatisfied, and if satisfied, how satisfied on a scale of 1-10. But there is another level, because we've learned that a customer can be totally satisfied and not return (and make a future purchase at a competing company). So, companies that 'get it' can see an additional dimension to customer satisfaction and therefore have a different customer service objective, one that goes beyond merely satisfying a customer. And if it can reach that higher objective, it gives them a strategic weapon that they can use against their competition to grow their market share.

This next level, 'exceeding customer expressed expectations,' requires the staff to go beyond what one might call the standard level of customer service. In order to operate at this level, it might involve making a few internal operating procedural changes, like increasing employee empowerment to have the authority to resolve any customer issues that may come up. There might also be an extra effort needed or an added cost, but the payback is increased business and further improved customer satisfaction. Take a hotel guest request for a 5pm late checkout. The customer knows checkout time is noon, and probably has an expectation that either the request will be turned down, or a late checkout fee will be imposed. Making an exception, by granting[32] this simple request will be a positive in a number of ways. It not only exceeds expectations, but gives the customer some insight into the customer service culture of the company. It also gives the customer an idea of what might happen next time they make a special request. Or, if something might go wrong next time, they have a better feeling that the company will make it right. All these customer feelings and impressions, based on exceeding customer expectations, are what builds customer loyalty. But what if you don't know what the customer wants?

Level 4: Anticipate/Satisfy Unexpressed Needs: Satisfying unexpressed needs of a customer is more complicated than operating at the other 3 levels. Not every need or want that a customer may have, will have been expressed or even thought of, and there are a variety of reasons for this. Many individuals don't express their feelings well. Or they simply don't want to ask or don't know to ask. In fact, beyond some basic set of expectations, they may not even be consciously aware they even have any particular additional needs. They also may not be aware that there is even a product or service that you can provide, beyond what they asked for. That's correct. Level 4 involves 'mind-reading' of sorts. Everyone has wants and needs, and letting you know what they are, gives you a chance to satisfy them. But at Level 4, guess-work is involved. But it's not all a guessing game, so empower and encourage your staff to have some fun with it. You know what similarly situated customers have wanted, and you can make suggestions based on your experience with other similar customers. Organizations that understand and try to anticipate and satisfy unexpressed needs, can create a lasting bond between themselves and their customers

Level 5: The 'Wow!': Exceeding Customer's Unexpressed Needs: In this 5th and highest level, the challenge is that the employee is basically operating in an environment where they have to anticipate an unknown and exceed it. So, if you're operating in Level 5, the 'Wow!' level, you have to guess and then use your creativity to 'surprise' the customer. You have to use the situation, your knowledge and experience, along with using customer non-verbal and visual cues and clues that are there, but not always obvious. (Or, follow the advice of Sewell and Brown: "Don't guess what they want, make it easy for them to tell you)."[33]

And perhaps most importantly, you need to develop and use your creativity and imagination in your discovery process. But to help you operate at Level 5, you do have some insight into the current customer and the situation they are in. Plus, you know what products or services you have available (or can get), in an attempt to exceed an unexpressed need.

So, meeting and exceeding unexpressed needs seems harder, but in a way, it's easier too. You see, at the initial levels, if you try and don't satisfy an expressed need, you may not have a happy customer. Level 5, the 'Wow!' level, is different. If you choose to operate in this level, all the basic and expressed customer needs have been met. If you try to satisfy or exceed an unexpressed need and fail, there is a good chance that the customer will recognize the effort as a positive. In fact, it may even encourage the customer to offer additional information to help you discover the previously unexpressed need. Where before, customers may have been reluctant to express the need, now, encouraged by your efforts to exceed their basic needs, they may offer some idea, some little bit of information that can stimulate your creative problem-solving ability and your imagination, and use that information to everyone's advantage.

Examples of Level 5: 'Delight, Surprise and Wow!'

'Good service is good business.' While it may be true, you'll need more than just desire and a clever marketing slogan or corporate pronouncement, if you want to 'delight, surprise and Wow!' your customers. As they say: 'You need to put your money where your mouth is.' Here's an example of how the 'new' General Motors has evolved.

In the past, General Motors Co. didn't systematically monitor social media and other websites for customer complaints. Now, the company has 25 to 30 people assigned to that duty full-time, says Alicia Boler-Davis, who was head of GM's global quality and customer-experience activities, and now EVP of Manufacturing. "We're engaging in over 8,800 unique interactions every month," she says. These range from congratulating new owners to explaining confusing technology or features, or responding to complaints about a defect or a breakdown. Boler-Davis says GM is giving customer-service personnel and dealers more latitude [translation: Empowering them] than in the past *to use GM money* [emphasis added] to resolve complaints and subsidize repairs on the spot. The main reason why a car dealer and car maker would go beyond the written limited warranty and extend what's known as a "goodwill" repair, is to foster brand loyalty in a market where most consumers feel none.[34]

Other Level 5 examples:

- Customer purchases a dozen roses, and you give them a small chocolate gift or something else of value that is not in the ad, and is totally unexpected.

- Similarly, at most bakeries, if you order a dozen bagels, you may receive 13. It's known as a 'baker's dozen' and the manager I spoke to said it was one way of thanking customers for their business.

Then there's the story of Edi at Mike's Auto Repair in North Hollywood, California and my old 1973 Monte Carlo. During a recent scheduled auto service visit, we discussed six items that needed repair, and the cost, which I approved. But later after I had left, as his technician was working on the car, he saw I didn't have a windshield wiper arm and blade on the passenger side and found one at a salvage yard and replaced it. He didn't have to 'spoil' the 'surprise' because he didn't need to get my approval for the expense. There wasn't one, because he didn't charge me. I didn't mention it when I brought it in for service (unexpressed need), because the car was over 40 years old, and the original part long ago discontinued.

A word about setting expectations. They have been set by other auto repair services I've used in the past, that have told me what they can and can't do, and charged me for everything. I was satisfied with the work to be done and the price I would be charged, and would have picked up my car and left a totally satisfied customer. But he operates his business as a Level 5 business in this higher 'delight/surprise/Wow!' realm, and it's the reason I drive past more than 20 auto repair shops on my way to see Edi and his team.

So, if delivering this level of service is proven to build loyalty, why doesn't everyone do it? Dyan Machan, a contributing editor at *Barron's*, in a recent article, explains it this way: "To an outsider, that can seem like overkill; to businesses that practice it, it's more like an ingrained culture of integrity."[35]

So how do we get to Level 5? Isn't satisfying the customer, and exceeding expressed needs enough? Remember the goal is not customer satisfaction or even exceeding customer expectations. The end goal is loyalty. It's capturing with certainty, the life-time value of every customer. And, while creating customer loyalty is never a 100% certainty, those companies operating at Level 5 will have the most success.

We focused on service, but the same holds true of products. If the product is 'right' it is right in a number of ways. A *Lexus* is a great looking car, but how many buyers take into account the safety and reliability of the vehicle, the cleanliness of the service bays, the friendly and responsive staff interactions? They even have massage chairs in the service department waiting room. You probably have your own 'Level 5' stories, and I'd love to hear them.[36] But, how do you know if you are operating your business and providing Level 5 service? Easy. Aim to provide a product/service level such that, when the customer is explaining their experience with you or your organization, and providing the details in a later conversation with a friend/colleague, or in a social media message or blog, they add, "and then they even …"

What do you actually need to do to hopefully elicit that type of response? You need to exceed unexpressed expectations and 'Wow!' the customer, beyond what customers could ever expect, or could even imagine. How? That's where an assessment of the customer and the situation comes in. Use your creativity, imagination and your knowledge and experience, along with any other information you find, like non-verbal clues, and then create a memorable customer experience, well in excess of what they expected. It will be one of the ways the 'Give Yourself A Number' process can be used to help you operate as a Level 5 business, when we discuss the GYAN process later in the book.

But there's another proactive skill you can use too. You can help 'set' customer expectations, by 'managing' them.

Manage Customers' Expectations

Obviously, improving the service level you provide can increase customer satisfaction (recall that: Customer Satisfaction = Service received ≥ Expectations). But what about expectations? From a purely computational standpoint, and given the service level provided, 'reducing' expectations in the above equation will also increase customer satisfaction. But while 'lowering' customer expectations may not be such a good idea, 'managing' them actually can work to improve satisfaction.

Telling the customer what to expect can significantly increase his or her satisfaction. Just like when you try to satisfy an unexpressed need, trying to 'set' an expectation may or may not initially be acceptable to the customer, since they have their own set of expectations. But it can assist you in getting to the right customer satisfaction solution. How? First of all, customers will recognize your effort as a type of commitment you are making to them. Like when you tell a customer *when* you will return a call or get back to them. It's a promise from you, to not only get back to the customer, but in a specified amount of time.

For example, if you are a customer, which phrase would you prefer, when an employee needs time to get the information you requested:

> • <u>Choice A:</u> 'I'll get back to you within the next five minutes, either with the answer or the status of what I've found so far.'

> • <u>Choice B:</u> 'One moment please.' Or, 'I'll get back to you *as soon as possible.*'

If Choice A above is a better response than Choice B, why don't we hear it more often? It's because the employee doesn't know how long it will take, and operates under the mistaken idea that no answer or a vague polite answer, is better than one that they actually have to follow through on and keep the customer updated on their efforts. But with Choice A, if the time frame is acceptable to the customer, you are on your way to a higher level of satisfaction, and if it isn't acceptable, you have the start of a customer engagement dialogue that can lead to alternative solutions to the issue. With Choice B there is no dialogue.

The customer also has no information as to when they will receive a response. But the employee also has no information from the customer. Does the customer need the information immediately or is a week from now fine? While not revealed, the customer still has an expectation of when they need the information, and will base their satisfaction on whether or not the response is received when expected, even if the information is not shared with the employee.

Managing expectations can help create an issue resolution 'partnership' instead of the typical complaint/confrontation situation, while making it easier to get to a more positive customer satisfaction outcome. Not knowing what will be done to resolve a customer issue, creates uncertainty and anxiety. So, until the customer issue is resolved, there is uncertainty, for both the customer and the employee.

Another way to set expectations is to provide choices. Giving a customer a choice of possible alternatives empowers them, while also opening up a dialogue, something just an apology never does. And again, customer dialogue/feedback can help you get to an acceptable resolution, perhaps not even thought of, until additional information was provided during the two-way communication.

Finally, you've probably heard the phrase, 'under promise and over deliver.' Your goal to improving customer loyalty should never be to under promise. I suggest it's to understand what the customer's needs are through dialogue and engagement. Once you understand what the customer's needs are, make a commitment to provide that level of service, and then over-deliver.

Employee Training: 'Vital Behaviors'

Before hiring someone to fill a job opening, organizations look for certain traits in candidates. The candidates then go through extensive screening and reference/background checks. Finding the right person for the job can be a very challenging assignment. Depending on the importance of the position, some companies hire third party expert recruiters to do the detailed search and research to find the right set of candidates to choose from. Others take a more analytical or scientific approach, and try to create a psychographic profile of prospective candidates. But there's also a simple thing you can do to increase the likelihood of selecting the right fit, when looking for new customer-focused employees. In my experience, it's very difficult to train an unhappy or unfriendly person to be happy and friendly. So, one shortcut I've used successfully, is if you have to choose between the two, hire attitude over experience.

After the hiring decision has been made, orientation and training follow. It may not always be the case, but here are a few scenarios I've seen, that can negatively impact your customer satisfaction delivery. For example, when business slows and costs saving initiatives are introduced, customer service training, is often viewed as an expense to be controlled. Also, lengthy new-hire training is generally rare. The reason is that by the time someone is hired for the position, it's usually been open for some time, and being short-handed has caused overtime expenses and may have reduced the overall service level. So, there's a need to get the new recruit in action and productive as soon as possible. The result: the newly hired employee starts out interpreting the customer's needs and deciding on the service to be provided, based on their own notion of customer service.

So, the new-hire is pushed into their new responsibilities early, while customer service training takes a back seat to the demands of day to day imperatives. Supervisors rationalize this, by considering it to be On the Job Training (OJT). What's so bad about learning while you work? Well, the OJT reality is that the employee 'learns' their new job by having their supervisor and others point out their mistakes.   Discouraged and demoralized, the new hire withdraws, afraid to make any more mistakes.

That's where cartoon punch-lines like, 'I'm sorry, but satisfying you is against our company policy' comes from. But it's no laughing matter. Without an investment in customer service skills and empowerment, cautious new-hires default to reciting policy and offering apologies for the inconvenience, instead of providing customer service solutions. Then the supervisor considers it leadership to criticize everyone for their poor customer satisfaction scores.

While the above scenario does occur, it doesn't describe the majority of situations. Remember, as with the concept of customer satisfaction, which is achieved by listening and then taking the right actions, employee customer service training is a means and not an end.

The end goal is a loyal customer, achieved through employee interacting with customers after they have received the proper orientation and training. Customer satisfaction, as we've discussed, can be complicated, so be careful not to overwhelm. With the individuality and the complexity that customer interactions bring, it's easy to overload frontline employees with rules, regulations, and corporate policies.

Instead, focus on a few key attributes you want to emphasize initially. You can't change behavior by focusing on every possible customer interaction. A million customers potentially bring a million unique situations. And, not only do customers have uniqueness but employees have unique talents and experiences as well, which all potentially conflict with the ideal of consistency in terms of customer satisfaction.

The authors of *Influencer,*[37] suggests that positive improvements can be made if we focus on the few vital behaviors that drive success. What are these behaviors that are essential for every customer interaction?

<u>The Nine Basic Vital Behaviors:</u>

1. Pleasantly greet every customer
2. Smile
3. Make eye contact
4. Identify yourself by name
5. Use their name
6. Offer to be of assistance
7. Acknowledge and welcome back returning customers
8. Ask if anything else is needed
9. Always thank them for their business and invite them to return

The above can serve as an outline of the basic components of every customer interaction.

After the basics are mastered, you can also add:
- Try to identify and anticipate customer needs
- Find ways to make customers feel important (because they are)
- Accept responsibility when things go wrong (even if it isn't your fault)
- Give the customer the benefit of the doubt
- If you get a request, do everything you can to honor the request

People on the frontline of a customer situation play the most critical role in the outcome of the customer's experience. Customer service training helps to make sure they know what to do and say to make that customer's experience a positive, pleasant one.

Investing in the 'Internal Customer'

We've discussed how some organizations view employee training as an expense to be controlled. But fortunately, most companies see training and related expenditures that are focused on their employees, i.e., their 'internal customer,' as a way to invest in the future of their business.

An effective training process should have three basic components: orientation, job skills specific to their position description, and then tie it all together with customer service training.

Orientation. Proper new hire orientation can help get the new team member off to a good start. With proper employee orientation, anxiety over expectations is reduced and so is employee turnover, according to Judith Brown, who explains, "Organizations that have good orientation programs get new people up to speed faster, have better alignment between what the employees do and what the organization needs them to do, and have lower turnover rates."[38]

Job Skills. Next is training in the skills required for the job they were hired to perform. But be sure to include the experiential component, tailored to the level of customer involvement specific to the job.

Customer Skills. The overall goal of training should be to make sure everyone knows their role in the organization and how to do the basics of their job well. Then, it is up to the leaders of the organization to create an environment that allows customer loyalty to flourish. They do that as they inspire and motivate the staff by example, encouraging every employee to make the right customer decision.

Being a top tier customer focused organization requires a consistently followed, 'top to bottom' alignment of all training processes. The format should follow the basic hire/train/motivate model, with leadership visibly demonstrating the right customer decisions. It's how you can ensure that the right customer focus is part of everything that makes up your corporate culture.

In his book, 'It's All about Service,'[39] Ray Pelletier discovered what makes great customer service companies and great teams so successful: great leadership. He discussed the important impact that leadership traits, such as vision, character, belief, ethics, collaboration, and enthusiasm, have on customer service. He concluded that when leaders display those traits, they inspire them in their people. As a result, their staff takes better care of customers.

What about companies that, in addition to focusing on customer satisfaction, focus on improving employee morale? Like customer satisfaction, as it relates to customer service, higher employee morale is better than lower morale. But also, as with job satisfaction of employees, it appears to be a necessary but insufficient predictor of their loyalty. We'll discuss the difference between customer satisfaction and customer loyalty in the next chapter, and as you use the suggestions in later chapters to improve customer loyalty, consider that those same approaches can be adapted to improve employee loyalty as well.

What You Want to Do vs. How You Do It

"I'd love to change the world, but I don't know what to do. So, I'll leave it up to you."

-Alvin Lee, writer, singer, British Blues Rock Band, "Ten Years After." (1971).

What do customer focused companies want to accomplish? The 'what' is a level of customer satisfaction (like Level 5) that leads to customer loyalty for the products and services that they offer. The 'how' (as in how to consistently deliver Level 5 customer service to every customer by every employee every time), is the difficult part.

Why is it difficult to write a customer service training manual that can be effective in the multitude of customer situations that can come up? It's because we don't know the future situations that the customer service agent will be in. We don't know what the customer is going to expect, say, or do. We don't know the future situation at all.

So why not tell employees exactly what they should say? The dilemma facing customer service trainers is that the more specific the customer service training guidelines get, the less likely they will apply. And, the broader the guidelines, the less helpful they are to the specific customer situation.

So, we get: 'Customers are our *Priority One.*' If trainers keep it vague with good sounding guidance but not specific to possible customer situations, the employee is left to self-interpret and decide the best course. Employees faced with the fact that their training is general in nature, but their tasks are specific, use their 'own good judgment' to determine service delivery levels, and that in and of itself leads to inconsistencies.

As a result, in situations where customer service staff may meet an almost infinite mixture of customer experiences, expectations and reactions, most training materials tend to be general in nature and lacking specifics. But while this may satisfy most, it is ultimately designed to leave some customers with unique expectations unsatisfied.

The Truth about 'The Apology'

Every customer service manual I've read, states that one of the first things the employee should do, when realizing the customer has a complaint, is to apologize. An apology is a statement of regret, saying basically, I'm sorry (that happened, or you feel that way, etc.). The customer is probably sorry it happened too, (whatever precipitated the complaint). So, there's regret all around. How important is receiving a statement of regret from an employee, when a customer has a complaint? Relatively speaking, receiving an apology is somewhat better than if you have a complaint and the employee is indifferent or hostile. So, on an improvement scale, it's probably a positive number, but it's a very small number. In percentage terms, it's 1% or 2% better than not receiving one. So, if an apology is all you plan to do, be prepared to lose customers.

From the customer's perspective, the only real good thing about receiving an apology, is that it sets an expectation. This is based on the assumption that when someone is aware that the organization they represent created a problem, a statement of regret is an indication that some positive corrective action may be taken. The customer doesn't know what will be done yet, or if what is planned will correct the problem, but an expectation is created. The mere fact that someone expresses regret however is meaningless. The real customer need at this point, is to know what specifically will be done to right the wrong.

In addition, from a customer satisfaction viewpoint, requiring employees to offer apologies, can be a negative. This is because for some companies or employees, giving an apology may make them feel that the apology itself is the solution, or apologizing is all they plan or need to do. At best, it's better than nothing, but unless something tangible is done to correct the situation to the satisfaction of the customer, the apology sets the wrong expectation. As we mentioned, some companies go even further with statements that sound good, but have no real meaning to the customer. I've heard employees apologize, and then add, "…and I'll make certain that it doesn't happen again." Sounds like something logical to say, but the customer is more concerned about the potential solution affecting them right now, than whether or not some future customer is similarly inconvenienced.

Anticipatory Solution Satisfaction

Anticipatory Solution Satisfaction is anything you do to create a pre-purchase commitment that gives the customer an indication that if the product or service doesn't end up meeting expectations, the customer will ultimately be satisfied with the final outcome. It's telling the customer in advance, that they can trust the product or service to meet their needs.

Warranty: Manufacturer's initial post-purchase warranty is an example. It's designed to let the purchaser know that the manufacturer or the seller stands behind the product. It gives the buyer/customer confidence that the benefits they are hoping to receive from the product/service they are buying, will actually occur, and if it doesn't, it lets the customer know in advance the terms and the details of how any 'service recovery' will be handled.

It's good when a company stands behind its product and lets you know up front. But what if you offer a personalized/customized product? What if you could get a commitment from the actual person preparing/making the product you're buying? At Starbucks™ it's called the Barista Promise: *"Love your beverage or let us know. We'll always make it right."* And then, put it on the cup the customer gets from the employee. They clearly get the Anticipatory Solution Satisfaction concept.

Return Policy: Like a warranty, your return policy is a visible upfront communication of an organization's service recovery process if something goes wrong. As a reflection of your organization's Anticipatory Solution Satisfaction culture, it can help get you from Loyalty to a Loyalty Bond with your customers (we'll discuss the importance of the concept in creating a Loyalty Bond later, in Chapter 5). To your customers, your return policy plays an important part in how the customer feels they might be treated, if something goes wrong. Some companies try to set that expectation of service recovery by having a 'hassle free' return policy, and then add the qualifier, 'some restrictions apply,' which tends to subtract all the advanced goodwill the return policy tried to create in the first place. You can easily get a quick insight into how the companies you do business with value you as a customer by comparing their return policy with others on the basis of just two metrics: Is there a cost associated with a return, and how long do you have after purchase to return the item?

- The Good: No fees, free shipping on returns, long return period
- The Bad: Brief return window, hefty restocking fees, exchange/store credit only
- The Ugly: As is: No returns, no refunds

But be careful, as marketers and their lawyers spend a lot of time crafting the 'fine print.' Examples of disclaimers abound, particularly when companies pick partners, but then don't stand behind what their partners sell to their customers. Take for example the 'Marketplace' a 3rd party seller section on the bestbuy.com website, which was discontinued by *Best Buy* as of February 24, 2016.[40] It was set up so you could buy items on their online 'Marketplace' from their partner/sellers on their website. But *Best Buy* gift cards couldn't be used to make a purchase. And Marketplace items cannot be returned to *Best Buy*. From their website: "…you must first contact the Seller directly with any issue on a Marketplace order. If, however, you are not satisfied with the response from a Marketplace Seller, you may submit a request with *Best Buy*

Marketplace customer service. We will *attempt* to resolve the issue on your behalf."

So, if your company has an 'easy to do business with us' culture, (and every successful company should), make sure that it's properly reflected in your return policy, all up and down your sales and distribution chain, including your business partners.

<u>What about 'The Guarantee'?</u> So, what about the promise of a 100% money back guarantee? If viewed properly, it really does two important things that have nothing to do with actually providing a refund. First, it's a before the fact, pre-purchase commitment to the customer, which is clearly a positive thing for the prospective customer. But setting the positive customer expectation upfront, creates an incentive (although somewhat negative) for the staff, that they must provide an excellent experience, or the consequences of having to give a refund may be reviewed with them at a later time. It's putting the employee, pre-customer interaction, in the position of understanding that if they are unable to satisfy the customer, their supervisor will need an explanation of why the guarantee was invoked.

But secondly, it's empowering to the customer. I'm not saying that every customer interaction is viewed by every employee as a power struggle, but sometimes that's how it feels to a customer, particularly if something goes wrong. With the employee holding all the cards, the guarantee helps level the playing field. The customer knows upfront, that they can always ask for a refund, and perhaps more importantly, the customer also knows that the employee knows that too.

Hampton Inns™, is one of the first brands to offer an up-front 100% guarantee, which has been in place since 1989. The guarantee itself is simply stated in just 16 words:

> "If you're not satisfied, we don't expect you to pay. That's our commitment and your guarantee."[41]

Can customers abuse the customer service guarantee? On the one extreme, there have been situations where the hotel internet didn't work, and the customer was given a full room rate refund, even after having had a good night sleep, and having enjoyed their free hot breakfast for their family of four.   Some customers have used the term 'slimy,' 'excessive', and 'embarrassed,' to describe how they themselves felt when complaining about some minor item, and then getting the charges for an entire night's stay removed.

At the other end of the extreme, significant problems have occurred, and no remedy or refund was offered. Hampton Inns™ may have a corporate policy but the brand is made up of mostly independently owned franchise hotels, who they rely on to implement their guarantee policy. Not unlike any situation we are discussing, no matter how good the policy, or no matter how well it worked in the past for you as a customer, if it is inconsistently applied, because of the uncertainty that it will be available next time, its benefit as a builder of customer loyalty is diminished.

But, in general, in situations where the customer is covered by a publicly known and stated service or refund guarantee, the customer outcomes are better. The service the customer receives is better, and the customer is more reasonable, since they don't have to make demands or exaggerate their claims of their unhappiness, because both sides know the guarantee is in place.

Guarantees are good, but they're not perfect. Like an apology, it may not resolve the problem or may not lead to a satisfied customer. If a once in a lifetime event is ruined, little is accomplished by a full and complete refund.

Talking about refunds, the employee may have in the back of their mind, that if they give them their money back, that will satisfy the customer and stop their complaining. It may satisfy some customers, but others are expecting the products/services they paid for.

The employee may think that giving their money back resets the experience to before the transaction for the customer, but it doesn't.

In that situation, employees without the proper customer service understanding can get frustrated, as they gave them their money back, and the customer is still unhappy. The employee may not understand why, especially if they view the transaction in financial terms rather than loyalty terms. In fact, many customers walk out of a business, even with their refund in hand, and promise to themselves that they will never come back.

Besides, if you 'guarantee satisfaction or your money back', it's really a misnomer. Guaranteed satisfaction means just that. It means taking the time to determine what satisfaction/benefit level was anticipated, and finding a way to provide that same level of satisfaction utility in a similar way. It may not have anything to do with a refund.

Finally, a guarantee may have little or no effect on the real important outcome of the interaction, and that's future customer loyalty. As mentioned, while the employee may feel a full refund is the solution, the customer may just think that things are going to go wrong again next time, and even though I'll get my money back eventually, it's not worth the hassle.

But the news is not all bad. Prospective purchasers of your products and services generally sees an offer of some type of guarantee as an insight into a company's customer service culture, and is helpful when they are choosing among alternative businesses. It also encourages customers to bring service failures to management's attention, providing an opportunity for customer service recovery, as well as ongoing operational improvement.

In addition, with the offer of a guarantee, the customer has an idea of how they will be treated if they need additional assistance or have a complaint. This assurance of knowing in advance what might happen if something goes wrong, is a very important component of the customer's future purchase decision process, and will be further explored when we discuss the Loyalty Bond.

Chapter Summary
Even the best rated customer service organizations may not be able to explain what they do specifically to be successful. Customer satisfaction is difficult to quantify, rating level feedback may be unreliable, and measurements of customer satisfaction is generally after the fact. The Five Levels of Customer Satisfaction (Figure 3-1) allows organizations to determine what level they operate in, and then set goals for further improvement.

And, the increased use of adaptive technology, smart device applications, and the proliferation of social media, is creating an opportunity to actually have a dialog with your customers over multiple channels (email, sms, voice, etc.) at multiple times (for example in hotels, pre-stay/in-stay/post-stay), benefiting both the customer and the providers of the product/service, helping improve the level of customer satisfaction they provide.

Finally, as we explore solutions to customer satisfaction and loyalty, the process and techniques discussed in this book, can be effectively employed across the full spectrum of customers, both external and internal.

PART II

CUSTOMER LOYALTY

Chapter 4: Defining Customer Loyalty

"The happier your customers and employees are, the more successful your company will be."

The *Cult of the Customer*, Shep Hyken, (Wiley and Sons, (2009)

Is Customer Satisfaction Enough?

There isn't a company or organization in the world that doesn't talk about the importance of customer satisfaction to their future business success. Everyone wants happy customers so that they will return, creating an ongoing stream of future value. But is having happy customers or satisfied customers enough? In a recent job posting on the web, a company was looking for a candidate that could *'ensure a high level of Total Customer Satisfaction* (TCS).'[42] Is that what the company is looking for? Do they know how high 'high' is? Does the candidate know how to 'ensure' it? Is 'total customer satisfaction' the ultimate goal of the company?

Is a Perfect Score Good Enough?

While it's true that a happy customer is better than an unhappy one, it's not always true that they will be loyal (repeat/return as a customer and advocate to others about your product or service). A customer that gives you the highest rating in all categories is indicating that when the product/service level received is compared to their expectation level, the mental equation result is positive. Expectations were met or exceeded. And, if you add to the equation price paid for utility received, you can get an idea if the customer feels they received 'value.' There is no indication in the data however that the customer will return as a customer. That's why the concept of customer 'loyalty' is important.

Using Only Satisfaction Scores to Predict Repeat Business

When we were doing our customer feedback research at Hilton®, we looked into the question as to whether 'satisfaction' (with a most recent stay) led to future repeat business. The data we were gathering showed that the higher the satisfaction level, the more likely the customer would return, but it wasn't always a direct relationship, and it wasn't always consistent, either within the brand, or for the particular rated property's location. A pro-active hotel General Manager in Chicago conducted the following informal experiment to try to empirically validate the relationship between satisfaction survey results and repeat business.

He created a list of customer names that had rated the satisfaction level at his hotel a '10 out of 10' during a previous six-month period. Then, using historical credit card data that tracked customer names by geographic spend for the subsequent six-month period, he looked for matches. He found a customer that had given his hotel a 10 rating in October, and stayed at a competing local hotel in November. The manager called the customer, and the conversation went like this:

GM: "Hi, I wanted to call you to thank you for staying at our hotel in October. I understand on our customer satisfaction survey, that you rated your stay with us a '10'."
Customer: "Yes, it was perfect. I was totally satisfied with my stay."
GM: "Great! Have you visited Chicago since you last stayed with us?"
Customer: "Yes, in November, I stayed at another hotel."
GM: "But you said you were totally satisfied at our hotel."
Customer: "That's true, I was. But I thought I might be even more satisfied by staying at the Chicago Hyatt®."

Once validated with similar customer feedback, it became clear that customer satisfaction is a moving target as new products/services evolve and customer expectations continually change. The conclusion: While individual customer satisfaction can be measured, quantified, and analyzed, a high customer satisfaction score does not guarantee repeat business or customer loyalty. And when aggregated, the ability of customer satisfaction ratings to predict future business trends is likewise limited.

The Customer's Perspective-Making a Repeat Purchase

The next component of our analysis of what makes up actual customer loyalty, attempted to determine the relative strength of the 'loyalty' the customer feels towards the product/service in terms of its importance in making a re-purchase. It's the notion that, given the expectations established by the image/advertising of the brand, as well as recommendations (colleagues and social media research), and the customer's own prior experience, the customer has or creates a set of established expectations about their future purchases. As a result, the customer 'estimates' how likely their expectations will be met during the next interaction with the company or its brands. The estimate may represent the certainty with which the expected value/utility they will actually receive will exceed their expectations. It attempts to answer the question: 'What will my experience be next time, and will it be 'worth' the price to be paid?'

Everyone who has ever been a customer has their own mental data base of experiences to gauge and estimate what their experience will be if they decide to make a subsequent purchase. The problem for the customer considering their next visit/purchase, is that they know it 'might' be the same, but more than likely, it will be different than the last experience. It probably will be better or worse, but it's unlikely it will be exactly the same. The customer may also factor in rewards, pricing, discounts, or other inducements in deciding whether or not to be 'loyal' in terms of the next purchase.

Customer Satisfaction vs. Customer Loyalty

Experience has shown that while it's true that bad customer service can lead to customers not returning, good customer service is no guarantee that the customer will return.

But repeat business is a critical a success factor, as it leads to sustainable, future revenue. Ongoing repeat purchases can also improve future profitability. One example is that initial customer acquisition costs can be spread over a longer customer revenue stream. Talking about customer acquisition and customer retention, you've heard a million times before, that it's easier (and cheaper) to keep an existing customer, than to find a new one.[43] You see them return, you acknowledge and welcome them back, and you thank them for their business, by making sure their expectations are exceeded. In the words of W. Edwards Deming: "Profit in business comes from repeat customers; customers that boast about your product and service, and that bring friends with them."[44] So it became clear, that while customer satisfaction is an important factor, it's just one factor.

High customer satisfaction appears to be a necessary, but not sufficient indicator of repeat business. So, we set out to look for other factors at work in addition to the customer's satisfaction with their purchase. We compared ratings received on several key survey attributes from multiple guests during their previous customer visits, to see if there was a relationship to future return visits. Our research at Hilton indicated that when asking about satisfaction levels, by adding additional attributes, we could improve the correlation between the customer feedback and their likelihood of repeat/return purchases, and help bring us closer to a working definition of Customer Loyalty.

Defining Loyalty

Satisfaction, Likelihood to Re-purchase, Likelihood to Recommend

Satisfaction: Depending on the customer's particular situation and set of wants and needs, when developing expectations, customers may consider several factors such as, price, service, convenient location, quick delivery, wide selection of service level choices and options, courteous and friendly service, and a customer-friendly return/refund policy, among others. Assuming their feedback is honest feedback, all these factors are taken into consideration, when you ask them anonymously, if they were 'satisfied.'

Likelihood to Repurchase: So, given that the customer received an acceptable level of benefit (customer satisfaction at least meeting their expectations), what other factors are at work that determine whether or not a customer will make a repurchase? The repurchase decision involves the customer making an assessment of how satisfied they were with the level of service received in the past. Then, they estimate the likelihood that that their satisfaction level will be as good or better than it has been in the past, and, decide if that level of satisfaction will be sufficient to make a purchase again. Also considered during the repurchase decision process, is a separate but related concept of 'defection,' which is the assessment of their likelihood or reluctance to switch to a competitor. It's their evaluation of how likely a competing product or service will bring them to a higher level of satisfaction or utility than what they are currently experiencing and will experience with your product/service next time.

For the hospitality industry, while many companies assume satisfied customers will be return guests, we found a significant number of satisfied customers, when asked if they would return, said they wouldn't.

Obviously, there are 'once in a lifetime' trips/vacations which by definition do not carry a return intent. But beyond these instances, the customer still looks at the 'return intent' response much differently than the satisfaction question. It appears that their quest for even higher satisfaction levels at alternative properties was at play. So, their 'intent to return' was clearly a separate attribute to be considered, in addition to their 'satisfaction' with their previous stay. This encouraged us to look for additional dimensions to help discover and define their reasoning, and be able to get to a more complete definition of Customer Loyalty.

Likelihood to Recommend: Customers also made a further distinction between they themselves returning, and whether or not they would actually 'recommend' the hotel to a colleague or friend. Customers that explained this 'advocacy' dimension of Customer Loyalty (sometimes referred to as Net Promoter® in the literature), usually spoke of their perceived 'self-image' and of the respect others held for their opinions. One interviewed guest said, "I'm putting my personal/ professional reputation on the line, when I tell a business associate that they should use that product or service." And we also found that there were many highly satisfied guests that upon reflection, even though they would return, wouldn't feel strong enough to recommend. So, it appears that this so called 'word of mouth,' advocacy/ recommendations were not given out casually. We found only truly exceptional experiences stood out enough in their mind, for them to indicate a high score for 'likelihood to recommend.' We concluded that customers giving a high score in this attribute further increased the predictability of whether or not they could be considered 'loyal' customers.

So, in summary, the key Loyalty questions on our customer feedback questionnaire became the following:
- As you look back at your visit, how **satisfied** were you with your stay?

- If you were to return to the same city in need of hotel accommodations, please indicate the **likelihood that you would return**[45] to this hotel.
- Please indicate how likely you would be to **recommend** this hotel to your friends or colleagues.

We found that adding these two additional overall attributes (intent to return and likelihood to recommend) improved the reliability of predicting if a satisfied customer will in fact make a repeat purchase. This helped us attempt to define and quantify 'Customer Loyalty.'

Defining Customer Loyalty

Customer Satisfaction

Likelihood to Re-purchase

LOYALTY

Likelihood to Recommend

Figure 4-1: The Three Components of Customer Loyalty

The graphic above serves as a visual description of the three components of loyalty, and their interdependence. This helped us with a working definition of Loyalty:

A 'Loyal' Customer is defined as a customer that is: totally satisfied with the product/service/value received, will state that in a similar circumstance, that they will make a repeat purchase, and were so impressed with their overall experience, that they would recommend their friends/associates become a customer too.

Differences in Customer's Value

"All animals are equal but some animals are more equal than others"

George Orwell, *Animal Farm*, (1945)

Customer Segregation/Stratification

All customers are valuable, but are they 'equally' valuable or are some more valuable than others? Of course, we know that some buy more or spend more or do so more frequently. There are many that believe that the Pareto Principle, often referred to as the '80/20 rule' applies conceptually to customers. This principle suggests that 80% of their business (revenue or profit) comes from the top 20% of their customers. But even if the 80/20 rule doesn't always apply, unless all your customers contribute the same profitability, every business has some type of an 'importance' hierarchy or statistical distribution curve ranking their customers, with some on the top, some on the bottom, and the rest in the middle. And this information can be used to create opportunities, rewards, and incentives for each segment, which leads us to the discussion of so called 'Loyalty' Programs.

Loyalty Programs

Loyalty Programs (also Loyalty Marketing, Frequency, Recognition, or Reward Programs) are a strategic customer tracking approach to marketing, in which a company focuses on growing new and retaining existing customers through incentives, separate from the quality and pricing of their product or service offering.

In the U.S., one of the first Loyalty Marketing Rewards program began, when Betty Crocker Baking Mixes issued coupons with their product that could be redeemed for baking dishes and related items. Later, expanding the concept beyond a link with a single product/brand, S&H Green Stamps developed a popular retail incentive reward coupon process in the 1930s. Typically, as a consumer shopped at various grocery markets, gas stations, retail and dry good stores, they would receive a set number of Green Stamps based on the amount of their purchase. The notion was to increase the customer spend at member retailers that were part of the incentive program. Retailers/Sellers were charged a fee to distribute Green Stamps and Customers/Buyers would paste the stamps into booklets and redeem them for gifts and prizes. Obviously, some customers would redeem larger amounts of stamps for larger, more value prizes.

The next logical iteration for Loyalty Programs was to identify, target and track those 'repeat' shoppers by assigning them a unique identifier, like a membership number. Then, along with their profile and preference information, use the information to deliver targeted, personalized services. These repeat customers who did, in fact, spend more would receive rewards, thereby increasing customer loyalty among those who are the more frequent customers. This tracking led to the ability to identify the very best of these repeat customers, so some type of special recognition could be provided to those at the very top. The information could also be used to create an engagement incentive for those at the bottom (or those not participating at all) to become more loyal. That's what the 'tier' designations within these 'frequency' programs attempt to do.

But a word of caution: Be careful about what message the gold/silver/bronze etc., label you use, sends to your employees. 'Low tier' customer identifiers should be viewed by the employee as the next potential upper tier customer, and not just a way to indicate where to step down the service level. It takes a high level of training to develop a talent to make every customer feel like they are in the top tier. And, the occasional upgrade for an entry level customer, not only gives them occasional special recognition, but equally important, gives them a glimpse of what might come. In fact, customers being aware that they are not an elite status customer, when treated as one, will usually thank you by increasing their own level of loyalty.

Therefore, look for ways in your own business where the lowest tier customers can still be made to feel important and be recognized. Caesar's Entertainment® Hotels & Casinos handle this by designating their entry level tier as 'Gold', despite having three tiers above that: Platinum, Diamond, and Seven Stars. And, if the regular check-in registration line is long (or the premium registration area is empty), they will often invite non-elite guests to their exclusive top tier registration lounge to pick up their room key. This speeds the check-in for the non-elite guests who remain in the regular line, but at the same time gives those chosen for the enhanced check-in, the experience of what might be available if their spending increases.

Loyalty programs are designed to reward repeat business, but an ancillary benefit is that they provide recognition. Being recognized as a returning customer, conveys certain privileges and helps increase the likelihood that their needs will be met if something goes wrong.

As far as a loyalty program's effect on 'loyalty,' if the primary target is the business customer, (or expense account holder, or any transaction where the purchase decision is made by the person receiving program benefits, but that person is not paying for the good/service), they will tend to be less price sensitive. If the customer is spending their own money and has to pay a higher price to receive program benefits, (given the availability of similar alternative products/service levels at a lower cost without benefits), their purchase decision factors in the implicit cost of the 'perks.' Therefore, for self-paying customers, the effectiveness of these programs in generating incremental repeat business is lessened.

An unintended consequence of Loyalty Programs is that they may create a pricing differential with competing products/services that can offer lower prices, since they don't have the expense of a frequency program. Companies then need to decide whether or not they should compete on price, or whether the advantage of having a loyalty program is strong enough to justify its cost and potentially higher pricing. Usually, the answer is to focus on both: customers motivated by incentives and those focused on price. Determine what is driving the purchase decision through qualifying preference questions to the individual customer. Then, utilize every incentive and pricing tool available, in order to maximize 'the spend' for that particular customer or customer segment at that particular moment.

Other retail programs like those offered by grocery, electronics or office supply retailers, offer program points and sometimes discounts or coupons not available to non-program participants. For example, Starbucks® charges a small fee for coffee refills, but doesn't charge if their pre-paid loyalty card is registered (complete profile and provide email address), which allows them to not only track customer spend, but to offer loyalty points and other marketing incentives to members.

Usually the cost of the program is built into the price of what they bought in the first place, and redemption of the reward is generally limited to products/services available through the issuing company, and subject to redemption restrictions. Also 'breakage,' (points that expire or are never redeemed), tend to somewhat offset program liabilities and expenses.

Membership fee shopping clubs like Costco® exclude non-members, and provide access to member only special pricing, which is another example of benefits associated with membership. And recently, some retailers and restaurants have started issuing gift cards that offer discount pricing in return for exposure aimed at increasing trial, while being able to sell their product/service in non-traditional outlets. An example of this would be a $100 restaurant gift card, sold to a customer for $75 by Costco, which only paid $50 for it. A classic win, win, win.

In addition to incentives to make repeat purchases, and recognition of higher value customers, a third advantage of customer loyalty programs is in developing an ongoing communication relationship with the customer. Along with keeping track of your spend (dollars, miles, points etc.), comes monthly or quarterly communications statements, which provide an opportunity to not only thank customers for their loyalty, but to communicate bonus offers and exclusive personalized incentives to members along with their account statements.

As for your best customers in terms of spend, it may be helpful knowing, for example, those who have become less frequent recently, allowing marketers to customize incentive offers. Increases in the lifetime value of the customer and reduction in the likelihood of brand defection, as well as system-wide roll-up of category spending patterns are additional marketing research benefits.

Do Loyalty Programs create 'Loyalty'?

Is repeat business the same as loyalty? They both indicate a desire to make a repeat purchase. But to say loyalty programs create 'loyalty,' is a myth. The definition of loyalty involves more than just frequency. It's a commitment to make a purchase, sometimes irrespective of price or convenience, because of prior satisfactory experiences, and a positive assessment of how well the product/service offered is expected to meet their needs. This 'loyalty' is what creates a willingness to make ongoing purchases, despite the availability of competitive and substitute items. And as discussed, loyalty suggests a willingness to recommend and advocate to others to make a similar purchase.

Loyalty Programs in contrast, basically encourage a customer segment, focused on the incentive rewards, to make a purchase that they might or might not normally make. Which brings us to the question of the day: "Do loyalty programs create loyalty?" I think the best that can be said, is that they create 'forced' loyalty.[46]

Fundamental to any reward program, is the requirement that they offer incentives to make a re-purchase. But they're not fool-proof success stories. For example, infrequent or smaller volume customers may never vest to a level where they earn benefits, and large volume customers may vest in several competing programs which, in both instances, limit their effectiveness in driving incremental business. Add to that the fact that some employers that reimburse the employee/customer for their purchase require 'points' to be returned back to the company that paid for the products/services, (so the company can use the program rewards to offset its future travel expenses, for example), and their effectiveness in creating frequency is further reduced.

But somewhere in-between the never vested and the multiple program players is the 'sweet spot' for reward programs. These programs are most effective where similar substitute products are similarly priced, from competing companies that are available in relatively similar circumstances. For example, where airlines with similar airplanes, service levels, routes, airports and arrival/departure schedules compete, one with a rewards program and one without, those with a program can drive incremental business from their program participants providing they remain price competitive.

When products/services associated with frequency programs charge a premium, either because they feel their frequency program benefits make the buyer more price insensitive, or to offset the added costs of the program, prospective purchasers make an additional mental value calculation. They compare the added incremental cost over a substitute non-reward program product/service, and compare that cost to the value of the benefit/reward they will receive by purchasing a participating product. If the value received through program participation is greater than the incremental added cost when compared to similar non-program products, they make the program related purchase. If it isn't, they don't.[47]

Other than start-up costs, which can be substantial, there are generally no other barriers to entry. So once competitors develop competing rewards programs, the early adopter advantage tends to be reduced, especially if later entrants raise the benefits. So, in addition to competing on price and product/service, now companies needed to compete on program features and rewards as well.

Starwood Hotels (now part of Marriott) was a case in point. In the hotel industry, Marriott was the first to create 'Marriott Rewards' with Hilton following closely with its Hilton 'Honors' program. Starwood was late to the party. The price they paid for late entry? They were forced to offer benefits that far exceeded the competition, along with the associated increase in program operational expenses. But by doing so, the Starwood's Preferred Guest Program attained instant credibility and critical mass for their program. They offered 'no blackout dates' for reward redemption (The goal of blackout dates is to try to minimize the impact of 'free stays' displacing paying customers during high demand periods). The reason they had to add such a costly program benefit is that early entrants have early participant vesting, which, by design, makes switching brands more difficult, unless there is a clear reason to do so.

Their competition, reluctant to raise the internal costs of their program and displace paying customers during high demand periods, didn't match the 'no blackout' program benefit right away. The Starwood's strategy was so successful, that in just 18 months it had over 5 million members, and was being recognized by frequent travelers as the best loyalty program in the industry.[48]

When everyone in the industry has a rewards program, the early adopter competitive advantage is no longer sustainable, with reward/frequency programs becoming one more attribute on which to compete.

The point of reward programs is to have the customer purchase decision be made, not just on the basis of price, product, location, and service level attributes that businesses traditionally compete on, but also by factoring in program rewards into the purchase decision process. And for the purpose of our discussion on loyalty, to in effect, take customer service levels out of the purchase equation. No one starts a reward program, so they don't have to focus on customer satisfaction. But the fact is, that the most ardent program players will purchase a product or service even knowing the service level may be lower (or the price higher) than other equally available substitute purchases.

In addition, it may be an unintended consequence, but companies with reward programs may actually put less emphasis on customer satisfaction. This is because customers vested in reward programs tend to tolerate lower service levels (and sometimes anticipate it), because of the offsetting program benefits they receive. In fact, vested customers generally rate service levels lower than non-program customers in the same circumstances, indicating that they might not have made the purchase, had it not been for the program benefits they receive.

Companies in a competitive industry probably view reward programs as a necessary evil. If a company offers one, the others are generally required to follow suit. In addition, program reward 'points' act as a type of substitute 'currency.' Points can be 'spent' to 'purchase' things. But, they can also be bought, sold, exchanged, and given away. And just like any third-world currency, the exchange rate for points can be devalued by higher redemption levels that can be introduced at any time.

Ultimately, however, true customer loyalty is a more powerful factor in determining whether to buy or not, even stronger than the lure of a reward. Reward programs may just lower the bar on what service levels customers will tolerate. Perhaps more interesting than instructional, but it appears that, when looking at hotel customers and the three attributes that make up customer loyalty, the expectations of reward program participants are opposite directionally to the non-reward 'once in a lifetime' dream vacation customers, as the following table shows:

Customer Expectations

Attributes of Loyalty	Reward Program Stay	Once in a lifetime Stay
Satisfaction	Low	High
Likely to Return	High	Low
Likely to Recommend	Low	High

The bottom line is that these reward/frequency programs have created a unique type of customer, one who might say, "I hate this place and so should you, but I'll be back."

Chapter Summary

Loyalty is much more than a customer being satisfied. To be considered a 'loyal' customer, three attributes are required: high satisfaction with the product/service, a willingness to repurchase and advocacy. A better name for the so called 'loyalty' programs might be reward programs, since participants in these programs need not be satisfied with the product/service, and may not even recommend it to their contacts, but still repurchase, due to the program benefits received.

Chapter 5: How Customers Decide To Be Loyal

Apart from the impact of 'forced loyalty' created by reward programs on frequency/return business, how can you tell if a customer will be a reliable return customer, i.e., what really is loyalty?

Well, an expectation of 'satisfaction' of wants and needs is a fundamental requirement for loyalty to even exist.[49] So why isn't total satisfaction enough to ensure loyalty? The expectation that the product or service a customer is considering will satisfy their needs is a prerequisite, but other factors appear to be at work. Every customer, whether new or making a repeat purchase, starts the purchase decision process with a set of expectations. The more experiences, good or bad, a customer has with a brand, product, or service, the more likely they will know what to expect. And the more reliable the personal experiential database, the better decisions they can make when deciding whether or not to be a return customer.

But expectations change. And competitive forces and technology are constantly working to develop new products, services, and better ways to improve the satisfaction of your current customers. So, as we learned in the previous chapter's example of a customer that was totally satisfied but didn't return, customer repeat business is still at risk, if they feel they might be even more satisfied with a new competitive product or service.

Given the customer's unique set of expectations, customers make a decision to purchase based on the probability that their needs and wants (their expectations) will be met. To help determine if their expectations will be met, the customer uses their own personal experience and that of others, including feedback from non-vested colleagues. In this way, it improves the likelihood that the correct purchase decision will be made.

And today, this so called 'word of mouth' feedback is not just limited to 'talking' to the prospective customer's friends and acquaintances. Social media feedback expands the customer's perspective and can ultimately impact both the company's brand and its profitability, as customers evaluate and use this shared outside information overlaid against their own experiences and expectations, in evaluating their future purchase decisions. These additional factors at work tend to be even stronger than the customer's link to rewards programs, which as we mentioned tend to reduce defection, but do not engender loyalty. And in this new environment, where consumer comments abound on social media, a clever advertisement won't get consumers to buy what other fellow consumers say is a bad product.

True loyalty, the kind that ensures that the customer will return and promote your business, comes in many varieties. Apart from your product or service, it can come from a brand, or a location.

Loyalty to a Brand

There are many reasons to brand an item. From a company's perspective, a brand's ultimate purpose it to generate pricing power. (Ask yourself if you sell artificially colored, flavored, sugared, carbonated water, and don't brand it, can you charge as much as Coca-Cola®)? Branding is also used to set customer expectations. Generally, a brand represents an image and a set of attributes that helps define what characteristics the product or service associated with that brand will have in the mind of the consumer. They can be real or imagined, tangible or intangible, they can be impressions of quality (good or bad), and they can be false. A brand's very name may impart an impression that may or may not be an attribute of the end product, like when Best Buy® was accused of price gouging during a recent natural disaster.[50] Shouldn't the Best Buy Company, really be a 'best buy' and not just call itself that?

But whatever attributes that define any given brand, implied in the concept of branding is the idea of consistency. The expectations set by the brand attributes and levels of service are expected to be consistently available, regardless of the location, time, price, or other variables. When a product or service represented by a brand is inconsistent, the brand is damaged, and its ability to maintain pricing power or drive repeat business is diminished as the anticipated level of quality for the product or service cannot be relied upon.

The brand image or tagline is intended to establish expectations of attributes that the product represents. If that then aligns with the customer's needs and wants, the likelihood of purchase increases. If you want something that quickly picks up kitchen spills, well, there's Bounty® the 'quicker picker-upper.' Or, you might be thinking this small container of fragrance is expensive, until you hear: L'Oréal® Paris, 'Because You're Worth It.' You can think about your own top 100 brand created expectations, but the point is, if you can create expectations, you have a better chance of meeting or exceeding them, i.e., satisfying the customer with your product/ service. Colloquially, you have probably heard Marketeers say: "we need to 'push' our product more." Simply stated, marketing, and branding advertising/promotions are the 'push' that help set expectations.

So, when you and your organization try to get and keep customers, you are trying to create loyalty. And to do that, you need to meet/exceed their expectations. And, to do *that*, you need to know what those expectations are. Then, and only then, can you work toward delivering against those customer expectations, to satisfy the customer, and create loyalty.

How can we tell if a customer is loyal to a particular brand? People can explain how loyal they are, but in the case of brand loyalty, actions speak louder than words. Some examples include, walking/driving past a competitive substitute good or service to get to the brand that is preferred. In general, brand loyalists will be willing to pay more, and incur more expense (time, money, inconvenience) to make a repeat purchase.

A brand represents a reputation, and companies spend billions of dollars to make sure it's a good reputation. They also spend billions protecting it by making sure no one tries to benefit or use it as their own. A brand is also a promise that the quality and attributes that define the brand will be maintained. The brand itself has intrinsic value separate from the products and services it may collectively represent in the mind of the customer. (In fact, it's usually listed as an intangible asset 'goodwill' on a Balance Sheet). If it's a good brand, (i.e., consistently delivering the quality level and utility that the customer is looking for) it helps the customer in the purchase decision. But like loyalty, it has to be nurtured and maintained at every contact point, and if it's lost or no longer trusted to represent the collective value the customer had expected, the image of a brand can be damaged, and then, it just represents a sign marker indicating a product or service to avoid, like the Tropicana® Brand example.[51] Delivering on the promise of the brand is vital to maintaining its value, and is the responsibility of everyone who represents a brand.

Then there's the so called 'halo effect.' Brand extensions are attempts to expand the appeal of the core brand to related products to a wider audience, like when a car brand adds a sub-model to the primary brand (*Toyota: Camry, Corolla, Prius*). But sometimes the primary brand may represent unrelated products, (*BIC Pencils, BIC Razors*). The concept being that if primary brand represents positive attributes, those attributes accrue to the brand extensions.

A lot of the feelings or impressions that brands emote are hard to quantify. Surveys can get opinions and relative rankings with substitute or complementary products, but ultimately the real definition of what the brand represents is a function of how the individual customer views its integrity.

Marketers need to make sure if brand extensions move the brand upscale or downscale, that it does not ultimately damage the core brand. Marketing practices also need to be monitored, to maintain the integrity and trust customers place in the core brand. Take the current practice of reducing the quantity of the product rather than increasing its price in some packaged food brand extensions. They even use the same size box/packaging, even if the quantity or weight of the product itself is reduced. These marketing practices can damage the brand's perceived value, and ultimately damage the core brand integrity, as customers feel cheated by a brand they previously trusted.

What about how measurement of the amount of the product is displayed? Expressing quantity by just saying 'ounces' is one of my favorite examples of how sellers can try to confuse buyers, since in the U.S., an ounce is confusingly both a measure of volume and of weight/mass. (Thanks avoirdupois).

If 'extra' soft Charmin® is better than regular Charmin, but you receive 1.568 square meters less product for the same price, customers need to do some serious calculations, as they re-compute not only the cost per unit of measure, but also the brand image and trust worthiness, in addition to its value proposition. (Product quantity to 3 decimal places designed to inform or confuse)? Marketers hope you won't pull out your calculator, but instead just buy the product, because they say meaningless things on their packaging, like: 'now, even softer', or 'family size,' or '10% more', (without telling you if the price per unit changed). What can end up happening, however, is the customer doesn't do the math. They just look at the deception, associate it with the brand and avoid the products they used to purchase consistently, as their brand loyalty and the trust value drops toward zero. And these days, customers once lost may never come back. Why?

One reason is the transparency of social media. In the past, private service recovery efforts to win back a customer after a misstep were private, between the manager and the customer. Now, social media has empowered customers, present and future, and has made it more difficult for a product/service provider to 'hide.' Take the following *Yelp* dialogue for example. The customer gave an initial negative review, and the manager intervened to win the customer back. As a result of the manager reaching out to the customer, the customer updated its initial review with the following notation:

"UPDATE: A few weeks after I wrote my previous review of [the no name hotel], the general manager called me to talk about my experience at his hotel. He explained to me that he was completely unaware of my situation and was apologetic. He even offered my husband and I and my husband's parents compensation to make things right. I did appreciate that and him taking the time to call and discuss everything with me. I think the hotel general manager deserves credit for that. That is showing more customer service than I received the first time around. Thank you. That was all I was looking for. With all of that said, I still stand by my previous review. I still refuse to return or recommend the hotel. I just thought I should let people know that they at least tried to remedy my situation and did the right thing."[52]

Service recovery is an art: there is no 'one size fits all' answer. The resolution of the issue, and restoration of goodwill can be as unique as the individual. As in the case of customer satisfaction, what satisfies one customer may not satisfy the next. In the above case, while it was admirable that the manager got involved, it's clear from the update, that the remedy wasn't enough to maintain the customer's loyalty (return purchase or recommend). Perhaps because the apology and the offer of reimbursement were their standard response (apology and refund). And, while what was offered, was done with the best intentions, it wasn't based on a two-way dialogue to get feedback on how to win the customer back. We'll discuss using the GYAN process to help in service recovery situations in Chapter 10).

Want another reason not to lose a customer in the first place? Once trust is eroded, any amount of advertising and sweet-talking tends to have little effect.   Any 'gain' you may have received from misrepresentation, is usually short lived. Further, it's also 'bad profits' according to Fred Reichheld, who states in his book, *The Ultimate Question,* "Whenever a customer feels misled, mistreated, ignored, or coerced, then profits from that customer are bad. Bad profits come from unfair or misleading pricing. Bad profits arise when companies save money by delivering a lousy customer experience. Bad profits are about extracting value from customers, not creating value for them."[53]

So just remember, your organization can create value for customers, but you can also take value away. The bottom line is that your customers are telling the story of your company based on their experiences. Make sure it's the story you want told.

Branding is a powerful tool in creating loyalty and generating repeat purchases. We covered the inadvertent damage that can be caused when the quality and service standards imbedded in the brand are not maintained. The conscious (or unconscious) violation of the 'promise of the brand' could end up destroying the brand, but not right away. Potentially, loyal customers will make one or more purchases after an unscrupulous company has decided to abandon brand standards in an effort to reduce costs or improve 'bad' profits, thereby reducing the value of the brand. In the long run, customers might no longer be loyal and could leave the brand, but in the short run, customers are paying for value they thought was there, but isn't.

Loyalty to a Location

Customers are discerning enough to know that even the same branded products may deliver different benefits and experiences, at different times and locations. Take a hotel brand. Hotel companies know which hotels within the brand are delivering at a service level below so called 'brand standards' through their internal inspections and customer research. It used to be their little internal 'secret.' Now, everybody, including prospective customers, know this information as well, thanks to social media and other public feedback sources, like industry ratings and the experience of their colleagues and associates. Sure, hotel customers hear the marketers touting the value proposition of the brand, but at the same time, realize that it's not always true everywhere and all the time.

Just like the case where brand integrity is damaged, customers get to the point where they can no longer rely on the brand as an indicator of quality and this 'lost loyalty' results in the customer never purchasing that brand again, even though most of the branded locations meet or exceed the customer's expectations. Lost location loyalty is a corollary of brand loyalty. If it's lost because of a relatively minor misstep, it's not lost for good. This is especially true if the customer has been loyal when a mistake occurs, since the higher the satisfaction/loyalty before the incident, the higher the likelihood the customer will give you a second chance. This is why an effective service recovery process is an important part of retaining 'at risk' customers. But there is an exception. Lose a customer because of an integrity issue, and all the inducements, discount coupons and 'we want you back' incentives are meaningless.

In fact, one of the major operational challenges for corporations that own brands is managing standards in a franchise environment. Franchising out your brand generates additional fees and increases corporate profits that wouldn't be available if you limited your business to only 'corporate owned and managed' properties, but carries with it risk. With independent owners responsible for the delivery of the quality standards, the brand image can be damaged, since the owner of the brand doesn't directly manage the property. For the hotel industry, 'The brand' lives at the 'macro' or system-wide level, but is enhanced, maintained, or damaged at the 'micro,' or individual property level.

For example, take the situation where a hotel customer is inconvenienced, and requests a refund. If they remain unsatisfied due to this incident (micro-level), they may associate the problem at the brand level and assume it may occur at other locations, and therefore may never return to that branded hotel regardless of its corporate advertising pronouncements or its locational global distribution (macro-level). The local franchise property has a different perspective. The customer may be a brand-loyal customer, but even when the experience exceeds their expectations, they may never have an occasion to return to that particular franchise location. If a problem occurs, the local manager may not want to incur the cost of a refund that would satisfy the customer, even though the service failure was their responsibility, because the 'cost' to maintain the brand loyalty is incurred locally, but the benefit accrues globally. From the Corporate Brand's standpoint, the often quoted 'boiled frog' analogy may apply, as marketers sometimes don't realize the incremental losses because they are so gradual (like the frog in the pot of water on the stove that heats up gradually), until the brand is damaged beyond repair.

At Hilton, we tested other customer focus criteria like locational loyalty (loyalty to a place regardless of the brands there), versus brand loyalty, (loyal to the brand regardless of location). While loyalty to a location was found to exist, it usually existed in the extremes (really liked/really didn't like a particular location). And, it seemed to only be relevant if it scored directionally different than the overall brand. For example, if respondents were shown to be loyal to the brand, this usually trumped location, and when there was no brand loyalty (or the brand wasn't represented in the desired location/destination), branding was less important than a particular location. While it was observed in the data, it was judged more of a breakdown of consistency of locational delivery on the various standards expected at the brand level. So occasionally, a customer would be loyal to the brand, but have a particular problem with a specific hotel, so we counted it against the location but not the brand. Less frequently, a customer would not like the brand, but favor a particular hotel location.

In either case, they were considered exceptions, certainly to be acted on, like potentially removing the location/property from the brand, but not significant enough to drive a global customer loyalty strategy.

The Math behind the Loyalty/Value Proposition

Brands are designed to set expectations. Each time a customer purchases the good or service represented by the brand, they evaluate whether or not these expectations were met or not. The mental equation they use to calculate the benefit received is: the perceived quality/utility received, compared to the service level/utility expected, or:

Product or Service utility received – Expectations = Satisfaction with utility received (+/–).

In this context, if the utility received was what was expected, the customer's expectations of value and customer satisfaction were met, and the numerical result of the equation is 0. Likewise, expectations can also be exceeded (service level/utility received is greater than expected), resulting in positive customer loyalty. Similarly, if utility levels received did not meet expectations, the result would have a negative impact on customer loyalty.

If their pre-purchase expectations are reflected in the price they are willing to pay, then, by comparing the net utility received to the price paid, the computation gets us to whether or not 'value' was received as a result of the transaction.

The math behind the loyalty value proposition, i.e., asks the question, was value received or not?

- Perceived Utility of Product or Service received > Perceived cost (price paid) = yes
- Perceived Utility of Product or Service received = Perceived cost (price paid) = maybe
- Perceived Utility of Product or Service received < Perceived cost (price paid) = no

A couple of notes: All of these metrics are 'perceived' and not absolute, (i.e., perceived value relative to what each individual feels is either a relatively high or low price). And since these are at the unique, individual level, based on perceptions, individual experiences, net worth, propensity to consume and historical experiences, 'value received' will be different for different individuals. And obviously, there are also costs other than the price paid that can be considered as part of the equation. That's why these equations should be viewed directionally, and are not quantified. And finally, the critical assumption used is that the higher the net value received relative to the price paid by a given individual, the higher their likelihood of advocacy and repurchase, and by extension, the higher their 'loyalty.'

<u>'Fair Price' and Perception of Value:</u> Pricing is important to both the company providing the product/service, as well as the customer/buyer.

To the company, setting a price for their product/service is one of the most challenging management responsibilities, since it impacts not only the business financials, but the demand for the product/service. In addition, it also needs to reflect not just the cost to provide it, but must anticipate the value provided, as well as the value expected by the buyer. Higher prices tend to generate higher profits, but only if demand remains the same or higher. As prices increase, the quantity demanded for the product or service tends to decrease relative to the perceived 'value' of the product or service, and its competitively similar substitute products and services.

The relationship between what you pay, and what you receive, is the price/value relationship. At pre-purchase, while the price and the perceived value may be known and represented by the individual customer's expectations, the actual value is unknown until received. In general, there is a direct relationship between price and expectations (the higher the price, the higher the expected value). While everyone's perception is conceivably unique, each individual making purchasing decisions will have a ceiling representing a price above which the price is deemed too high to complete the purchase transaction. On the opposite end of the price/value spectrum, is the floor. Even if priced at zero, the product/service could represent value or utility so low (or negative) that the transaction won't be completed even if it's free.[54] In between the maximum price and the minimum price, is where the purchase decision is made, based on the customer trying to maximize the positive difference between the value of the utility received, and price paid. The higher the difference, (utility > price), the higher the 'value' received.

How does all this relate to customer satisfaction and loyalty? Recall that 'price' is being used for our purposes as reflecting the customer's implicit value expectations. The lower the expectations, the easier it is to exceed them, and therefore easier to increase 'satisfaction.' The higher the expectations (created by 'perceived' high prices), the harder it is for the utility of the product/service to meet expectations, and therefore the harder to create customer loyalty.

But it's a little more complicated. For example, let's say a customer initially feels that they paid a 'fair' price for the value received and are 'satisfied' with the purchase. Then later, they find out that other customers received the same product/service level, and paid a lower price. This perception of 'fairness' can adversely impact satisfaction levels. According to David Messick's model[55] of how people judge fairness, customers quoted a price, will first weigh it against a personal norm, or the so-called reference price. Then they add expectation of value to be received, based on past experiences, knowledge of prices for similar products/services and filter all this information based on their personal perspectives.[56]

Customers generally understand that they have to pay a premium for the latest model or in high demand/short supply situations. But in general, while pricing impacts perceived value and therefore satisfaction with the transaction, understanding what product/service attributes a customer values, is also important. This is especially true, if they are given a choice of optional value-added features (free extended warranty, liberal return privileges, free shipping etc.). If these features are incorporated into the product/service offering, they can mitigate the 'fairness' issue in the mind of the customer, and improve the overall value received (customer loyalty) equation.

CRM and CEM

Customer Relationship Management (CRM) can be broadly defined as a system for managing a company's interactions with current and future customers. It often involves using technology to track, organize, automate, evaluate and synchronize sales, marketing, and customer service interactions with an organization.

Customer Experience Management (CEM) often provides similar functionality as CRM. But in addition, it focuses on the customer as a person, rather than simply a faceless client or a number in a database. The focus is on the individual customer's 'experience' during interactions with the organization:

- It helps organizations to look at itself from the customer's perspective.
- This allows the business to work toward providing the experience you believe your customers wants when interacting

with your organization, and helps incorporate your customer's thoughts and emotions in to the experiences you provide.[57]

Analysts and commentators who write about customer experience (CX) and customer relationship management have increasingly recognized the importance of managing the customer's experience. Every customer receives some kind of experience, ranging from positive to negative, during the course of buying goods and services. In their book on CEM, Thompson and Kolsky[58] say that "an experience is defined as the sum total of conscious events. As such, a supplier cannot avoid creating an experience every time it interacts with a customer." This suggests that providers create an experience for the customer, whether intentional or not, and customers receive an experience from the interaction, whether conscience or not.

So, while it may be a moving target, you need to be aware of the customer experiences you and your staff are continuously creating, and focus on managing these experiences to achieve the best customer outcome.

Keep in mind that the customer experience begins from the very first interaction, which may be the first phone or in-person contact, but it can also be your advertising, or your organization referenced on social media, or your website. For example, a poorly designed website, or an unanswered phone call or email, or even seemingly endless automated phone menu option prompts, can lead to lost business, even before you've had a chance to share your excellent products and customer services.

In a study designed to improve website usability for customers, Tealeaf Software Solutions (tealeaf.com) discusses using CEM processes to improve website experiences. They suggest that, "Visibility is the missing link between your business and your customers. In the context of Customer Experience Management, visibility is defined as the ability to see your customers in real time, every one of their unique interactions with your site, for every customer, every single time. If you can capture what the customer saw and did, and what your site's response was, you can fill the gap that exists today." They were analyzing customer interaction with a website. But what if, using the GYAN process, you could improve this 'visibility' in the real-life personal interactions with each of your customers in real time?

It was mentioned earlier when discussing surveys and guest feedback, forward looking companies are moving beyond the traditional after-purchase questionnaire to get customer feedback, and trying to capture feedback throughout their entire engagement with the customer. In the hotel industry, that would be, pre-stay/in-stay/post-stay. If customer feedback could be instantly captured through multiple channels made available by the proliferation of applications for smart devices that guests already wear/carry with them, customer service issues could be responded to more quickly, as the ability to interact, is always 'on.' Even if not always used, just the fact that the customer knows a direct link to your organization is always available to them when they need it, can improve the customer relationship and their experience, as both are maintained and managed in real time.

So, is the answer just gathering more feedback from the customer? Social media, text data mining, predictive analytics and phone, on-line and written surveys/questionnaires are all designed to determine what the customer wants, and their reaction to the product/service received, representing the tried and true concept of the Voice Of the Customer (VOC). But in and of itself, they are just a piece of the equation, not the answer. How many individuals, organizations, corporations and world-leaders have received excellent research data, studies and survey data, and have misinterpreted, misused, misunderstood or ignored the research? It's what you do with the information that counts. While more and better research is probably a good thing, at some point you have to do something with it, and unfortunately, the research seldom comes with a methodology to get the optimum result from using the data.

So, to summarize, if the new area of competition is based on delivering experiential value, measuring these attributes becomes the vehicle that matches up what you promise, with how well, what you deliver is received or experienced by your customer. This can then lead to operational improvements that can result in a type of 'Customer Experience Optimization.'

You may be doing the things you think the customer wants and performing them well. But from the customer's perspective, the relationship is under constant review and subject to constant change, for better or worse, due to the most recent experience they've had with your product or service. If you are able to manage how well, over time, your product and services meet the customer's wants and needs through their experiences, you are managing the customer relationship.

Foundational and Experiential Components of Loyalty

The customer's experience, which we're all trying to manage and improve, is a function of how well their expectations are met/exceeded.

Back in Chapter 2, we introduced the notion that customers have two sets of expectations as it relates to products and services they buy. The 'foundational' component represents the basic utility and functionality of the product/service. If it's a watch, how well does it tell time? If it's a delivery service, did the package safely arrive when expected? Foundational expectations are met, by answering the question, 'How well does it do what it's supposed to?'

Then there's an 'experiential' component, representing the 'feel' or the image the product/service projects and accrues to the buyer when they purchase or use it. So, once the customer assures themselves that the watch they are planning to buy tells accurate time, they move on to how will it look and make them feel, and what image (sporty, elegant, modern, hi-tech, hip, classic, retro) it will project for them.

Foundational: The foundational aspect of the products or services you provide is essential. If you're not doing those fundamental things right for the customer, the customer is at risk. But doing those things well is not enough to ensure loyalty/repeat business. We applied the often-used concept of necessary but not sufficient, when we said customer satisfaction was necessary for there to be loyalty, but other things had to be in place as well, like wanting to repurchase and willingness to recommend. The same is true when companies are focused on managing their customer's experiences. Foundational attributes are necessary but not sufficient. By adding and managing the experiential components (the 'feeling' and emotional aspects of how the customer experienced your product or service), you will have a more complete view of the product and services you provide from the customer's perspective. Take Disney® parks as an example of a laser focus on both foundational and experiential. The parks must be spotless and well maintained, or all the fantasy, excitement, and wonder they try to create would be meaningless.

Experiential: In the hotel industry, companies realize that things like cleanliness, courtesy and physical condition are important to maintain. But they are not items that distinguish a brand, or things that they can compete on. These are the basics, the foundational attributes. If you can't get those right, you can't maintain your customer base. What distinguishes hotels is the experiential attributes (like relax and re-energize, fun and excitement, accomplish purpose of visit, etc.).

When choosing a hotel, it needs to be convenient, clean, safe, and well maintained (foundational). If it's not, you're not going to stay there or return. But if it provides all those things, the deciding factor of 'which' convenient, clean, safe and well-maintained hotel you choose, will be based on how closely it will deliver the experience anticipated (experiential). Deciding if and when to make a purchase when you have no first-hand foundational or experiential knowledge can be strongly influenced by friend's and colleague's recommendations. But as we mentioned earlier, decisions can be based on the opinions of strangers too. Social media comments and reviews are an increasingly relied upon source. It doesn't ensure the outcome of 'your' experience, but it does help in setting 'expectations' and when cost compared to anticipated benefit is factored in, can lead to a decision to purchase or not.

The Relationship Between Advertising & Social Media

There is also a relationship between company advertising and social media. Both are designed to address foundational aspects of the product or service, while allowing the prospective purchaser to estimate/anticipate the experiential components, like meeting their initial expectations, or creating new ones. They both deliver messages that can influence customer purchases. The difference is directional. One comes from the company/service provider through its marketing communications, and the other from previous customers.

But is the flashy, attention grabbing, big budget marketing message true? According to a study from *Nielsen*, a leading global provider of information and insights into what consumers watch and buy, ninety-two percent of consumers around the world say they trust 'earned media,' such as word-of-mouth and recommendations from friends and family, above all other forms of advertising.[59]

Savvy consumers, initially enticed by a marketing message, often use external sources to validate marketing claims. Most marketing messages hope you'll assume the foundational aspects are in place and focus on the experiential. For example, restaurant ads seldom feature the results of their health inspection report in their advertisement, but instead, feature a lot of happy couples, enjoying champagne and sunsets from their ocean view tables. Contrast that image, with comments from independent and unaffiliated people within social media sites, who actually visited the restaurant.

Sharing their experiences can be a strong influencer, as is external direct feedback/review data, like results from industry leaders like *J.D. Power* or *Consumer Reports*. Together, the information can be useful in evaluating the accuracy of the marketing message, and help new customers decide if they should in fact, make a purchase.

Beyond Customer Loyalty-The Loyalty Bond

'What will happen if something goes wrong next time?'

Product/service providers, and even prospective customers may not always be consciously aware, but every customer preparing to make a purchase, estimates the probability of the company delivering on the promise of the brand. And, unless the confidence level is 100%, a corollary question most customers consider is, "What will happen if something goes wrong?"

Customers expect that foundational and experiential expectations will probably be met, but also realize that sometimes unexpected things can go wrong. If they feel their expectations will be met/exceeded, *and* if something does go wrong, that the resolution will also meet/exceed their expectations, then a "Loyalty *Bond*"[60] has been created.

A customer that has a Loyalty Bond with your organization assumes, with a subsequent purchase or interaction as a customer, that not only will things go well, but has the additional expectation that if they were to encounter a problem in the future, it would be resolved to their complete satisfaction.

The concept of the loyalty bond has two components: First, what is the degree of confidence that the customer knows how they will be treated if something goes wrong? And secondly, how satisfied will they be with the anticipated outcome?

This 'loyalty bond' concept provides a unique perspective. It attempts to give the customer an insight into *their* perceived value to the business as a loyal customer. Before their next purchase, the potential repeat customer tries to determine not only how the prospective product or service will meet their needs, but also how likely they'll be satisfied if something goes wrong.

It's almost as if the customer is asking themselves the question of leverage. If something were to go wrong, what will the customer be able to say or do to convince the staff to correct the problem? Are the employees empowered to resolve any issue that may need to be resolved? Will my past loyalty matter? Should it? Is the person I'd deal with if something went wrong, aware of my importance to their business, and do they even care? And, how much goodwill and future loyalty could be generated, when a particular customer that didn't have 'leverage,' is treated as if they did?

I realize these are a lot of rhetorical questions to ask yourself as a customer, but it gets to the heart of the area beyond what we traditionally consider loyalty and addresses the loyalty 'bond'.

It may sound complex, but it should be a very routine calculation for both sides; the customer and the business, centering on the 'life-time value of the customer' (past loyalty being one indicator) and the incremental 'cost' of resolving the problem (taking into account the local vs. global distribution of costs and benefits).

To summarize the two components of the loyalty bond from the customer's perspective, they try to decide: If something goes wrong, will I be:

<u>Treated Fairly</u>
1. Likely
2. Not sure/not likely

<u>Then, will I be Satisfied with the Outcome</u>
1. Likely
2. Not sure/not likely

Why is this concept of the loyalty 'bond' important? Most frequent hotel customers may experience variability of service delivery, but upwards of 90% have never experienced a situation that would rise to the level of a complaint. We previously discussed that before social media, complaint resolution was largely known only to the customer and the business itself. This fact used to put other potential customers at a disadvantage. But with social media, prospective customers can now gain expanded insights into how they will be treated if something goes wrong, by looking at the experiences of a large number of similarly situated past customers and how they were treated.

So, perhaps even more important than the current foundational and experiential outcome of a given product or service, is the notion of the customer having an idea of how they will be treated (what will happen) if they encounter a customer service problem in the future.

Obviously, if they've had a problem in the past, they know how it was handled good or bad, and how they were treated, and how they feel about the outcome, so they can add that to the database of experiences when making a future purchase decision. If they had a bad encounter, it may have been enough to make the customer not shop there again. Wait. Can one bad experience outweigh and cancel several good experiences? Yes, it happens all the time. In fact, in most customer transactions, customers feel at a disadvantage, somewhat powerless; until they consider their ultimate weapon, stop being a customer.

Perspectives on the Loyalty Bond

Earlier, we discussed how offering some form of a 'guarantee' has the added benefit of giving the customer some pre-purchase indication of how the situation will be handled if they will have a post-purchase problem. This represents a type of customer empowerment, because if you can give some early indication that the customer is likely to get any potential problems resolved to their satisfaction, it helps strengthen the loyalty bond they feel towards the product or service offered.

There are other ways that companies selling products and services can communicate to the customer a feeling of having additional leverage, if something were to go wrong.

Take the banking industry for example. Banks as a group, not known for their customer friendly perspective these days, are having a rough time convincing customers that their bank is really their 'friend and partner', like they say in their ads. Who wouldn't be skeptical, given the banking industry's perception problems? (Are bankers really sometimes called 'banksters')? What's a bank to do? How about this: What if, when dealing with a specific bank representative, you knew the name of that person's supervisor, and how to contact them directly.

And, you knew that information up front, before the actual transaction. It would not only be customer empowering but as we saw during our discussion on guarantees, both sides know the customer can invoke the escalation process at any time. The service provided will be such that in all likelihood, it won't be necessary to contact their next higher manager to get a customer's expectation met, or a problem resolved. At least that's the hope. Here's what I found at the bottom of an email, I received from a Bank of America® staff member: *"If at any time you do not feel that I am offering exceptional service, please email my supervisor (by first and last name) at (direct email address) for assistance."*

This access to the 'next higher manager' accomplishes a number of positive variables that are always present when customers interact with employees. And like the upfront guarantee, knowing the supervisor of the employee you're dealing with, empowers the customer should they choose to escalate if a problem occurs. But look at what else it does.

From the perspective of the employee, providing, the contact information of their boss up front to the customer they're dealing with, (not just some customer call center), motivates them to do whatever it takes during the interaction, to avoid the customer ever needing to contact their supervisor.

Further, it also encourages supervisors to delegate authority to those in direct customer contact. And perhaps most important of all, it helps improve the attitude of the customer contact employee. In my experience, most of the un-resolved customer complaints and ultimately lost customer business stems from employee arrogance, when the employee feels the customer has no recourse. (Customers always have the recourse to stop being a customer, but believe it or not, some employees don't always care about that either).

So, from the employee's perspective, the goal is simple. Make a customer feel that no matter what might go wrong, that you will make it right. If they could rely on that assurance, you would have created not only a loyal customer relationship, but a 'loyalty bond' as well.

Chapter Summary
Customer loyalty (satisfaction, repurchase, and advocacy) is always at risk as the marketplace and people's expectations are constantly changing. That's why to keep loyal customers, you need to maintain an ongoing customer dialogue, while measuring and managing the customer relationship. The simple math of customer service is: service level received – expectations = experience, expressed as positive, negative, or neutral. Adding price paid allows the customer to compute the value proposition of the transaction. Branding helps set expectations of service and value that will be received, forming the basis of loyalty.

But a loyal customer stays loyal only as long as their expectations (created by the brand, or invented by the customer) are continuously met/exceeded. Adding the concept of 'customer empowerment' helps create a 'Loyalty Bond', as it suggests ways that uncertainty over the next transaction's outcome can be removed, and the bond strengthened, when the customer not only knows what to expect when things go right, but also knows what to expect when things go wrong.

Chapter 6: Barriers To Customer Loyalty

We learned from the *Zogby* survey discussion in Chapter 1, that the number one company in terms of customer service was rated excellent by less than 62% of their customers, which is hardly a passing grade. Your company's score is less. Why is creating continuous customer loyalty such a mystery?

Well, first of all, there is no shortage of advice on the road to customer loyalty. Some of the greatest minds in the field have admonished companies over the past 30 years, to stay "close to the customer," and "listen intently and regularly to your customers and learn from them." The problem is, that well-meaning, and good sounding phrases that are designed to teach new skills, don't. They are vague, subject to individual interpretation, and don't accomplish what they set out to do. It's a case where the teacher knows the information in the lesson very well, but finds it difficult to convey the specifics to be learned in such a way that they can be understood, remembered, and applied by the student.

We've also described the challenge that organizations face in trying to decode what the customer expects in exchange for their loyalty. It's a challenge because customer's wants and needs are potentially unique to every one of them, and their expectations are continually changing; the proverbial 'moving target'. So, the situation is one in which the business doesn't always know what it will take to satisfy the customer, and the customer often doesn't know either. Now, if we look at it from the employee's perspective, the person expected to deliver customer satisfaction, delivering exceptional customer service has its own set of challenges for them. The following are a few examples.

The Authority vs. Customer Interaction Paradox

The fundamental problem starts with how a typical hierarchical American business is structured. This may not describe your organization, but typically, there is an inverse relationship between authority and customer contact. Usually, supervisors have more authority and more experience than front-line customer contact personnel. As a result, the higher up a person is in the organization, the higher the experience, and authority. The owner/president conceivably has unlimited authority and power to fully satisfy any customer. As you go down the organizational hierarchy, less and less authority is granted, yet exposure to customer interaction increases, to the point where, at least theoretically, the employee with the least experience and authority has the most customer interaction.

Experience: Let's take a look at the front desk of a major hotel. You'll find supervisors in the back, managers further back in offices, and generally the newest, least skilled, lowest paid, least empowered employee in full customer view. They have the least authority, and concerning customer service, have the most immediate initial responsibility. They are usually somewhat aware of the financial goals of the company (increase revenue and reduce costs) and unless they have customer goals as well, they enter the employee/customer arena with a financial perspective. So, as the agent is saying, 'welcome, how may I be of service', they are thinking: 'a request for a price reduction will reduce revenues and an extra toothbrush or towel will increase expenses.' As the customer makes their request, this is the filter that is usually applied.

Authority: The front-line employee usually operates in an environment where they have little authority to make decisions outside of their job tasks. So, sometimes the customer will ask to see the manager. But any attempt to get the manager involved can sometimes be viewed by the manager as an interruption by the employee: (why can't you handle this, can't you see I'm busy), (do I have to do your job too?), (how many times do I have to tell you: "NO!"). If that type of supervisor/subordinate work environment exists when the customer request exceeds the employee's authority, the front-line employee becomes a 'go-between', a negotiator. The goal for the front-line employee is really just to explain, in hopefully acceptable terms, why you, the customer, cannot get what you requested. If the employee is 'successful' the customer is usually unsatisfied, no matter how pleasantly they leave. The employee through rational discourse, and persuasive verbal, non-verbal or whatever other skills they have developed in this environment, has survived, has won. No negative financial impact and they didn't have to disturb the boss. If the employee isn't successful in convincing the customer that they don't need what they said they wanted, the result is the same: the customer is unsatisfied.

It may seem surprising, that with all the books and all the practical advice on the importance of authority delegation and empowerment, the reason some companies have low customer satisfaction scores can usually be traced back to lack of authority delegation to front-line employees. So, when the employee is told their number one job is to satisfy the customer, this operating culture can create a disconnect, between what the employee is told to do, and what they are able to do.

Why supervisors don't delegate authority may go back to the wrong notion that they've 'earned' their promotion, and 'paid their dues.' Supervisors may think, 'I've spent time in front-line customer service positions, and survived/escaped. I'm glad I don't have to do that anymore.'

We promote those successful at customer service out of customer service roles, and leave behind those less good at it. Spreadsheets, bar graphs, pie charts, email reports, presentations and other 'paperwork' on the other hand, may not be fulfilling, but it's what supervisors do, so it must be good. Supervisors also can tell people what to do from 'behind the curtain.' They can give orders that they themselves wouldn't want to follow, like telling you to decline a customer request for a refund for example, without their experiencing any of the negative customer reaction consequences.

In analyzing how to improve your own customer service culture, look for internal situations where your organization delegates 'responsibility' but not 'authority.' If you are trying to improve your customer outcomes, the last thing you want to have, is employees that are demoralized and frustrated, because they are not empowered to take care of the customer.

Karl Albrecht[61] once said, "If you're not serving the customer, you'd better be serving someone who is." And if he is right, (recall customers can be both internal and external), then every employee position description should include a discussion on getting to the right internal and external customer outcome in their specific role that the job they are performing is intended to accomplish.

Operator/Manager in Denial

It's possible that most of you reading this are saying to yourself, this doesn't describe my employees, in which case, everything is fine. But some may wish to at least consider the possibility that your company doesn't always create satisfied customers.

Perhaps you've seen customers unsatisfied, but you rationalize that it is usually the customer's fault. They don't understand our business. They complain all the time, have a bad attitude, and are too demanding. Of course, you know you would handle the customer properly, but you can't be everywhere, all the time, and you are not personally involved/aware of every situation.

Further, an executive's world is viewed through positive filters. For starters, employees are different when the owner or manager walks into the room. And, what happens when they ask their employees 'if everything is ok?' No matter what business you're in, there's a natural reluctance to bring bad news to the boss. The intention of the manager's question is good. You feel engaged, you're checking in with the team so you can assist if needed, etc. But in good or bad situations, your employees want you to feel that everything is ok; everything is under control. They're not looking at it as deceiving you, but rather as keeping things positive. For others, maybe they've seen messengers who were shot. And who amongst us hasn't put a 'spin' on information we've sent 'upstairs'? If you are a Vice President or General Manager, it's even worse. You almost have to disguise yourself or wear camouflage to get to see the real world within your organization. And please don't assume that information from above you is an accurate representation of the reality on the front lines either. They are more isolated from the everyday customer call or visit than you are.

Also, it's likely that you wouldn't have hands-on experience with most customers because you don't interact with common customer requests/complaints; your staff takes care of them. Putting on a name badge once a year during HR's annual 'trading places' team member event, (where you carry a piece of luggage, check someone in, or smile for the newsletter camera as you stir the soup kettle in the kitchen) doesn't count. And unless everyone is under video surveillance, you don't see everything. But, if you think a front-line employee is reluctant to tell their supervisor that they need help to satisfy a customer, how likely will the president get a request from the employee needing empowerment? And the manager and executives between the front line and the president view their informal position description as including the phrase, 'Keep complaints and bad news from traveling up the chain of command.' So, the further away you are on the org chart from the actual customer, the better things look. And it's all a secret. If the customer complaining doesn't care enough to escalate or gives up before they persevere, (try calling the president of any company with a complaint, and see if s/he takes the call) then according to the employees, given their constraints, they were successful.

So, is the solution as simple as giving employees customer satisfaction goals and empowering them, in addition to the financial perspective they already have? Yes, it is, but only if their supervisors have the same set of goals. If you see a customer satisfaction goal on the president's personal performance goals, it's an organization that values and will focus on satisfying the customer. Why? Because every employee is silently watching what their managers and supervisor do, not listening to what they say.

Also acting as a barrier to creating a customer focused organization, is the notion that the executives are 'driving' revenues and profits. It's almost as if customers are secondary; a kind of necessary evil. We need them, but we don't need them enough to change our management style. We're the ones running the company. After all, we as management set the strategies, we make the game plan, we 'drive' results, we 'call the shots,' we're in charge etc. Are they really in charge? Are they essential to the success of the company? If the manager left and the customer stayed, would the company still be successful? If they stayed and the customer left, would the business still be successful? The corporate egos and corporate arrogance exude from many successful corporations, but everything is a 'point in time.'[62]

'You're Wrong Either Way'

As an employee, have you ever found yourself in trouble, no matter what you did? Supervisors in this environment get very good at chastising employees. When the employee satisfies the customer, the supervisor tells the employee they shouldn't have had to give such a big benefit (refund, credit, etc.) to retain their loyalty. They weren't there so they don't know. At the other end of the spectrum, the employee follows the policy guidelines and doesn't satisfy the customer, and the supervisor criticized the employee for not contacting them so they could have properly resolved the issue. 'Empower, but not too much power' is a common game these supervisors play, and the customer service employee ends up in the middle. The result is that the employee is demoralized and now reluctant to give a concession to a customer or a refund for fear of being criticized by the supervisor. So, as it relates to the customer, the employee reasons that the criticism from the customer is less enduring so they end up apologizing, taking the wrath of the customer, and moving on. It's the classic 'no win' situation, a choice of the lesser of two evils, so the person that gives the employee their paycheck wins out, while the company loses another customer.

Everybody is a genius, and knows what to do after the fact. If you run a business and you have a supervisor like that, make a change before they do further damage to your customers and employee morale.

Employee Disdain for the Customer

One of the unsolved mysteries of life for me, is employee arrogance. It's an off-putting attitude that customers often run into. It's a mystery, because the customer is paying the bills and theoretically paying the employee's salary. It also conflicts with everything organizations say to their employees about customers. In fact, if we listen to companies talk about customers, (the customer is 'in charge', the customer is the real boss, the customer is always right), employee arrogance should never even happen. But it does. I bring it up here only because no one talks about it, and that doesn't mean it doesn't exist.

What causes arrogance in employees? Lack of self-awareness provides the right environment, but is not the cause. In my experience, it's more a reflection of the culture that the employee finds themselves in. It starts with the way new employees are trained. They are new, so they don't have the experience yet to know the best approach. Their customer service training usually involves being told the things they should do, like treat the customer with courtesy and respect, but once on the job, they end up learning the things that they can't or shouldn't do. The things they can't do are specific but the things they can do are discussed in general terms. This is because it's easier to follow a rule or restriction (check out time is noon, no exceptions) than it is to extend a late checkout and cause a potential scheduling problem in the housekeeping department. Therefore, what you can't do is explained and documented in rules, regulations, and Standard Practice Instructions.

But when it comes to customer performance goals, employees may have some vague notions, but are usually in the dark. It may be because organizations don't know how to be specific when it comes to something as imprecise and ever-changing, as satisfying a customer. "Failed bosses created mushy goals that employees found difficult to map into actual activity. As a result, the wrong things got done and the right things didn't."[63]

If you are a manager and run into a similar situation, what should you do? It may also be that the newly hired front line employees are talked down to by their supervisors, and talking down to customers may be a way of re-balancing their self-image. Whatever the cause, there is sometimes an internal conflict between the stated goals of being friendly and respectful to the customer, and the environment they work in. They are told, "Your job is to satisfy the customer." Yet there are so many rules and prohibitions and restrictions they must learn and enforce, that employees sometimes look at their job more as a gate-keeper between the interests of the business and the satisfaction of the customer. In fact, during one of my research interviews for this book, one front-line employee told me, "Most of the time, I have to break a rule, to satisfy a customer."

Also, look for correlations between what customers are saying about the inability to resolve their customer issue, and what surveyed employees say about the barriers they face when trying to satisfy a customer. Then change what you have to change.

Finally, if a customer has a complaint, it sometimes can become a power-play. Think about complaint resolution from the employee's perspective. They have all the power when it comes to customer interaction. The employee has the experience of knowing what the company can and will do when something goes wrong. They know the history, the internal rules covering problem resolution and the limits they and their supervisor will go, or not go, to satisfy the customer complaint, and how likely and how frequently exceptions to the rule are made. This arrogance probably isn't part of the overall business operating culture, but it may exist with some of your employees. A good indication it exists, is when the distribution of your numerical customers rating scores tend to skew to extremes.

I'm Right and You're Wrong

Observing thousands of interactions between customers and employees, it appears that sometimes, at some basic psychological level, some employees and some customers, carry around in the back of their minds, the notion of, 'I'm right and you're wrong.' A customer arrives later then the reservation, (someone fails to call the hotel to change the arrival time), and so someone is telling the other that they are wrong. The customer finds their soup too cold or their ice tea too warm, and so someone made a mistake, someone is wrong. Depending on the emotional stability of the people involved, anger and shouting can occur. While reacting emotionally or reciting the policy is easier, if the ultimate objective of the employee is a satisfied and loyal customer, that goal is not always met by doing so. Employees that focus on solutions to the issues, rather than how the problem is presented, will be more successful in their customer service dealings.

I'm the One in Charge

Similarly, in dealing with customer issues, this power struggle sometimes deteriorates as each side weighs the perceived power that they possess. Without the upfront guarantee or awareness of the other customer empowering strategies we've discussed, the ultimate leverage a customer has in the 'negotiation,' is for the customer to threaten to withdraw their future business. So, it's not surprising to me, after one negative occurrence, you may hear the customer say, 'I'm never shopping here again, and I'm going to tell all my friends." Sometimes the threat resonates with the employee, sometimes it doesn't. But it's a clear signal for those aware and focused on the life-long future value of that customer, that the customer's future business is in jeopardy.

While the customer is placing so much importance on the interactions with employees, the employee may not. Customer service staff comes in contact with customers all day, every day. There is a business risk that, from the employee's standpoint, handling customer issues will become routine. Employee's may become desensitized and may not view the situation with the same level of importance that the customer does. For example, I also hear from employees that feel customers tend to over-react when something goes wrong. When looking to explain this, I think it may be as simple as one side (the employee), doing a job over and over, and with so many transactions over time, they realize that occasionally things will go wrong. "Why should the customer over-react?" "What's the big problem?" The problem is, the other side (the customer in this single interaction) feels a commitment was made to them, a promise, and it's not being honored. The employee may have heard the customer issue or complaint a hundred times, but to the customer, it's a unique request. It's important for the employee to realize that, to the customer, they are representing the business and the brand, so every product sold represents a set of promises that the company is responsible for keeping.

Arrogance, or being obnoxious or aloof, in the context of customer service, is probably something you too have witnessed. Here are some of my recent observations:

Not My Job: Famous coffee cafe in LAX. I had just navigated a long line to get a coffee. The cream decanter was empty. An employee came out from back, peered out from a half-opened door and looked at the line. I asked her if I could have more half & half. She told me she wasn't working 'out front.' I asked her if she was too busy. She just pointed towards the person at the cash register and disappeared behind the door she was closing.

Customer Disrespect: At a local restaurant and after completing her meal, a woman handed the check and her American Express credit card to the cashier. The cashier without saying anything tapped with her pen, the little 'MC/Visa only' sign on the register, as she handed back the credit card.

Creating a Customer Friendly Atmosphere? At a nearby Los Angeles veterinary hospital, I checked in my pet and told the receptionist that my appointment was with Christine. In a terse, correcting tone, she said "Dr." (insert Last Name) will be right with me.

It may not always be on a conscious level, but your customers do evaluate or rate each contact with your employees every time they interact. They are judging whether the staff is being helpful or hostile, and will adjust the way they respond based on their interpretation of how they view the employee's attitude toward them. This is especially true on the telephone, where seeing you speak is not possible. This just means there is a heightened emphasis and importance placed on things like tone of voice, background noise, hold-time, and even their perceived phone 'attitude.'

Where's the Strategy for the Customer?

If you directly ask leaders of organizations if their customers are important, they will probably all say yes. This doesn't mean that they have clearly articulated their customer strategy to their team. We discussed earlier that statements about customers can be so grandiose as to lack specific actionable meaning for those that interact with customers. In general, the 'what' message is good sounding, but the 'how' message is absent. For instance, "Go the extra mile," or "Show them you care." Sometimes it's simple and straight forward. Treat the customer: 'right', 'well', fairly,' 'like family' etc. These are just feel-good statements that lack specifics, to the point where the recipient of the guidance may have no idea of how to fit the advice into their day to day customer interactions.

Sometimes, customer strategy is intentionally vague or only indirectly discussed. The idea being that if the organization does a few key imperatives well, like friendly greetings and welcoming smiles, positive customer experiences will follow. And some feel customers are fickle, demanding, and unreliable. Others feel if the price is low enough, a customer will buy, no matter how they are treated. And sometimes, the customers aren't even mentioned.

For example, I recently attended a senior operating officers meeting of a major company, where the President was outlining their roadmap to success. As the group was being told about the Key Performance Indicators to the company's future success, the following slide came up:

Four Pillars of Growth: Our "Four C's"

- Category Management
- Core 1700
- Cost Management
- Channel Growth

Figure 6-1: The Four C's

So, here is a billion-dollar retailer with stores in almost every state, and over 150 million customer transactions annually. Four 'Cs' and no 'C' for Customer.

If you asked the question, the response would be, "Of course everyone knows the customer is important." Maybe they do. But if it's so obvious, then mention it.

Or, it may be that customer relations management is so complex, and these other areas are so specific and concrete, that they focused on the key elements of growth that they could, in fact, explain, measure and manage.

Chapter Summary

In the previous chapter we discussed how customers decide to be 'loyal.' In this chapter we discussed how organizations, through their own internal culture, may say the customer is important, but how the leaders lead affects how employees respond to customers. And that can create barriers to achieving the goal of customer loyalty.

Customer satisfaction/customer loyalty is the key to a successful business, and it's the 'what' that everyone in the organization is trying to do. So, whether you're an organization that's trying to overcome internal barriers to customer loyalty, or you're an organization that has a good customer loyalty culture and wants to make it better, the next chapter will help. It will show you 'how' to do it, using the "Give Yourself A Number" (GYAN) process.

PART III

THE GYAN PROCESS

Chapter 7: Introducing the GYAN Process

'How' to Create Loyalty

I get the impression that the more people talk about the customer and what satisfies them, the less they really understand what to do, or how to do it. In this chapter, I intend to break the code. You and your team already know 'what' you want to do, and now, hopefully the GYAN process can assist with... the 'how'.

The 'what' (as in what we're in business for), is to be financially successful, and therefore work to maximize customer satisfaction and loyalty. Usually, the typical staff member or manager will be able to satisfy customer's requests, when there is an obvious answer. "I'd like more coffee/ok here you go, anything else?" Or in a hotel: I'd like an upgrade: "OK customer, I have 2 special rooms in my hotel... they both have great views and a nice balcony. One is available, so here's your upgrade." What you and your team do when there is no obvious answer, is what distinguishes employees, managers, and potentially your entire company from your competition.

If the goal of any customer/employee interaction is to have the interaction end with the highest possible customer satisfaction and positive impact on customer loyalty, one way to achieve this goal is by following the 'Give Yourself A Number' (GYAN) Process. It's a process that allows the employee interacting with the customer to gauge for themselves the level of satisfaction that their interaction will have on the customer in front of them, in real time. The GYAN process will allow you to be able to do this, despite the fact that your organization is staffed with employees with a wide variety of skills and experiences, and they face the uniqueness of each customer's wants and needs in any given situation.

Break the Code: The Customer/Employee Interaction

Have you ever been in a situation where you said something with good intentions, but it was taken the wrong way by the person you were speaking to? Well, just like in personal conversations, in every business interchange between an employee and a customer, there are a full range of words and phrases that can be used in any given situation. It doesn't matter if you are a food server, spouse, parent, child, manager, or CEO. The words you use as you engage someone at these communication touch points, will determine the feeling the person you are interacting with will have about the interchange. And in business, this feeling will define how they will look at you, and the establishment you represent, and use the information to determine if it will qualify for their future business and respect.   It will create a conscious or unconscious representation of your present and future relationship, and therefore help define their initial level of loyalty.

The thing to understand is that whether the customer becomes more loyal or less loyal, has little to do with the actual situation, like the service being too slow, coffee too cold, etc. The issue specifics of the interaction are not important. It's the impression that the customer walks away with, in terms of how they feel you view their importance as a customer, in the way you responded to these situations, that matters. You may think that you can rely on previous good experiences the customer may have had, to outweigh occasional missteps. Maybe, but realize that every new interaction has the potential to reset the customer's attitude and feeling towards the relationship from that point forward, and, for the better or the worse.

And communication is more than just the words you use. It's the non-verbals like tone of voice, eye contact, facial expression, gestures, and body language that will affect the outcome of the interaction. Finally, there is always the possibility that emotions will enter into a customer/employee interaction, which can bring the customer relationship much closer, or damage it.

The key is to be able to anticipate the customer need. But anticipating a customer's wants and needs are just a matter of trying to determine their expectations. This may seem obvious, but be careful. How many times have customers directly told you what they wanted or expected, and you just reacted to the question or statement, instead of taking the time to think through the situation both from your perspective, and that of the customer. On one level, something was said to you, and you responded. But on reflection, there may be something else going on, like a higher thought level that needs to be evaluated. Call it, Situational Awareness.[64]

Before you met the customer, they were just one of the multitude of people that are currently using, or thinking about using your product/service. Either way, you have no idea of what their current or future expectations are or will be. But that is exactly the information you will need to know to create a loyal customer. And, if you practice and use 'situational awareness' you'll be able to recognize not just what the customer said, but better understand what the customer's needs and wants really are. Then, you'll be in a better position to target your response and action, to increase customer satisfaction and build customer loyalty.

If this customer/employee interaction is so critical to the customer relationship and their loyalty, it's too important to leave its outcome to chance. So, how does the employee gauge the success of their current customer service effort?

Ideally what is needed is a quick, easily quantifiable process that allows the employee interacting with the customer, to be able to predict the customer satisfaction and customer loyalty outcome, as it's happening. This would allow them to positively adjust their conversation/ interactions in real time, with the goal being to make the customer leave the interaction with the highest possible positive experience.

If the 'what' you are trying to accomplish, is to increase your customer's satisfaction and their loyalty to your business, the 'how' can be achieved by using the 'Give Yourself A Number' process.

The 'Give Yourself A Number' Process

Let's start with a general example to explain the GYAN Process. Consider that while employees should have your company's customer service rules and regulations in mind, they should first, before interacting with the customer or saying anything, be encouraged to evaluate and understand the situation they are in (Situational Awareness). After starting off with a friendly greeting, a smile, eye contact, and a general offer of assistance, (refer to the vital behaviors, discussed in Chapter 3), consider using the GYAN Process.

The five components of the GYAN Process:

1. <u>Listen/Assess:</u> **Listen** carefully to the customer (paying attention to verbal as well as non-verbal communications) so you can **Assess** and understand the customer's issue or need.

2. <u>Plan/Think:</u> Then, with the **Plan** of exceeding the customer's expectations in mind, **Think** about the options you have and what you might say or do, to reach the intended customer outcome.

3. <u>Quantify/Evaluate:</u> Using your informal list of possible things you might say or do, pick one, by deciding what you are going to say/do. But before responding to the customer, **Quantify** the planned response you've chosen. 'Give Yourself A Number': a 'grade,' a self-generated score, on a scale of 1 to 10 in terms of how likely what you are planning to say will achieve the desired positive customer outcome. (From 1=very unlikely, to 10=very likely). Aim to satisfy the customer's issue or complaint, and provide a solution to the customer request, etc., all with the goal in mind to increase customer loyalty. Then, before doing anything or saying anything to the customer, **Evaluate** the response you are about to give. If your score is an 8 or more, go with it. If your self-assessment of your intended response is less, don't. Instead, think of a response that you can give that would result in a higher number, and say that instead. (This is the time for the employee to use their imagination, insight, talent, training, and experience and whatever authority they have, to come up with an 8 or higher response, and then respond to the customer).

4. <u>Respond:</u> Based on the number grade you gave yourself, if you're satisfied with what you are going to say (i.e., a score of 8 or higher), **Respond** by saying it to the customer.

5. <u>Observe/Act, or Re-Assess:</u> **Observe** the customer's reaction. You have just self-graded your response. Now it's time to compare this number grade you just gave yourself and determine, by observing the customer, what grade they just gave your response. If the employee feels the customer's reaction was an 8, 9 or 10, then **Act**. The employee will go ahead and do what their response indicated. If the customer's reaction is 7 or less, use the customer's reaction

and comments as additional input, and come up with a new response that you feel the customer will now rate an 8 or higher. If needed, **Re-assess** by thinking through the situation again. Use your skills, personality, training, experience, imagination, additional customer input, supervisor's authority; whatever it takes to come up with something else better to say/do, and repeat step 3 above until you're satisfied that what you will be saying and doing, matches your desired customer outcome.

Continue the process until satisfied that you've achieved the highest possible customer outcome.

If the interaction is handled this way, the employee creates a deeper situational awareness, and thereby, is not just reflexively responding, but managing the situation. By allowing the employee to estimate for themselves, how their handling of the situation will turn out in terms of a desired customer result, and using their own training, experience and creativity, the GYAN process can help them to maximize that particular customer loyalty outcome. How? With GYAN, it's all about the individual. Your job is to understand what the current customer in front of you wants and use GYAN to develop a way to deliver it in real time.

By anticipating the individual and their unique customer wants and needs in a customized manner (Situational Awareness), assessing the best response and then over-delivering, you can help ensure the products and services you're providing will meet the customer's needs. If done consistently, it helps morph the customer interaction process from convincing/selling your solution, to providing/exceeding the needs and wants of the customers. Fast assessments of needs and fast targeted responses can be developed as a talent. The quicker you can assess a situation, the better. GYAN puts you in a position where you can evaluate your response, based on how you feel the customer received it, to get you to the desired outcome. By practicing the GYAN process, you will develop a heightened sense of customer awareness and customer empathy. This can manifest itself in a multitude of ways, not obvious to employees not familiar with GYAN, who are just following procedures and reciting rules. It can help you assess the situation, think of creative alternatives to improve the customer experience, and then act.

I've seen servers anticipate that their customers may wish to share a dessert, and bring an extra plate and fork without being asked. Customer awareness and anticipating customer needs are difficult concepts to train, especially if you're just lecturing employees on following procedures. But it's an added benefit that flows naturally for someone using GYAN, since it's the awareness of/from the other person's perspective that makes this possible. So, to summarize the GYAN Process:

SUMMARY OF THE GYAN PROCESS

When a customer communicates a need: Practice listening carefully, quickly assess the possible solutions that will yield the highest/best outcome, and then craft your response to get the best outcome. Then, self-evaluate, how likely what you are about to say will achieve the desired customer result, on a scale of 1 to 10. It's that simple.

What's not simple is making the cultural changes within the organization that are necessary to allow the GYAN process to not only work, but flourish. We've touched on earlier why 'old school' supervisors find it difficult to delegate authority and empower front-line customer contact employees. For example, supervisors need to control the 'cost' of the potential service recovery solution. "We don't want an unhappy customer to get too much," I was once told, "as it might encourage more customer complaints, and increase our costs."

It's not uncommon for a 'financial control' mentality to be so pervasive, that it dominates/dictates the way front-line employees interact with customers. I could write a book on organizational culture and how changing it to a customer focus actually is the right 'financial control' decision/direction, but that's for another day. For now, realize that you can't 'cost control' your way to prosperity.

So how do you develop a 'customer focused' culture? Simple: create and foster an operating environment where employees feel that they can maximize customer loyalty without checking with someone first. Just the act of excusing yourself to get additional authority makes a customer think you don't feel that they are important enough to meet their needs without going to the boss. It also adds doubt and uncertainty to whether or not their needs will be met while you're gone, which can all be eliminated if you handle it immediately in the first place.

Want additional benefits from using the GYAN process? Well, implement GYAN at your place of business, and it will increase employee self-esteem and confidence, as their ability to improve customer satisfaction increases, when interacting with customers. And, overall employee job satisfaction will increase as customer contact employees can now resolve issues, instead of just apologizing, or checking with someone first. For employees, using the GYAN process can become a rewarding and enlightening experience, as they challenge themselves to come up with unique and creative solutions, thereby enhancing their customer and people skills. And this makes the job more fulfilling, as they can see the results in positive customer reactions that are a result of their actions.

And supervisors will now have additional time for more strategic decisions, as they will no longer have to 'grant power' each time a customer needs something.

It's logical, intuitive, easy to explain, understand and use, plus it makes good common sense. And, in my experience during GYAN group training sessions, it can even be fun and engaging, as employees open up and 'stretch their minds,' and come up with imaginative and 'wild' ideas, for both the 1s and the 10s on the GYAN scale. What's even better, in a 'brainstorming' session, it can be used creatively as a problem-solving technique, in a wide range of topics, in any type of customer situation. (See the next chapter's section on GYAN exercises and examples).

Using the GYAN process can allow you to differentiate your product/service from those you compete with. Take a photo of a guest room at a typical *Hilton, Marriott, or Hyatt*. Cover any logoed items, and you'll find that it is very difficult for prospective customers to tell them apart.

"Differentiate" is the marching order Doug Fleener,[65] a Lexington, Mass. retail consultant, gives his clients. Otherwise, he says, "you're just caught in a commodity war-- the kind of 'who's-the-cheapest' battle." But it's a battle you don't have to fight. Customers will pay a higher price for improved customer service. For example, according to Price

Waterhouse Cooper's® new 'Future of the Customer Experience' study, customers across a wide variety of industries, say that they were willing to pay as much as a 16% premium for better service (PwC:2018).

What's wrong with the way customer service is being handled now? A recent study by Strativity Group Inc., revealed that only 39% of corporate executives believe their employees have the right tools and authority to a solve client problems.[66] But with the GYAN process, empowerment, and senior level support, you can change this, and at the same time, create a competitive advantage for your business.

Using the GYAN Process: 1-10 Scale

Excellent customer service is so obviously a fundamental prerequisite of a successful business that no one would argue its importance. Yet so many companies fail to deliver customer service properly, while others seem to be able to delight their customers intuitively.

I mentioned the GYAN process can be used to evaluate a full range of situations, in addition to Customer relationships, so let's start out by trying to use the GYAN process's 1-10 scale to describe how companies might view customer service from their perspective:

Different views of Customer Service Using 1-10 GYAN Scale
1. There are organizations that don't think customer service is important or they can get along just fine without providing it.
2. Most companies fail to deliver it, but act as if they do, by paying it lip service. They say it's important, but don't want to go through the time and expense of making sure they deliver it.
3. Then, there are those that think it's important, but don't know what it is or how to deliver it.
4. Next, they think they have it, but don't/aren't sure how to measure it.
5. There are those that deliver it, but inconsistently.
6. Deliver it consistently, but at a mediocre level.

7.   At a consistently high level.
8.   Guaranteed, at consistently high level.
9.   Beyond customers' expectations.
10.   Create experiences that consistently result in a sustained customer loyalty bond.

This simple list of 1 to 10 is hopefully instructive in showing how the GYAN numbering scale process can be used in a variety of evaluation and decision-making strategic situations, as you work to determine what type of operational excellence and service level you'd like to provide.

Give Yourself A Number: Insights & Awareness

As we've suggested, customer service expectations are potentially unique to every customer interaction, as customer wants and needs are as unique as the individual that carries them around. And, customer wants and needs are sometimes hidden or not expressed, or not obvious, or may not even be consciously known to the customer themselves. But, and here's the secret, they can be estimated. And even when an employee aims high and misses, they can be close enough to get some additional feedback clues, and if in real-time, make immediate, positive 'mid-course' corrections.

And employees, when interacting with customers, have choices too. They can choose to just recite from the policy playbook. But even if it's a good playbook and has worked in the past, if you accept the premise that every customer interaction is potentially unique, the playbook won't always work, for every customer, every time.

With GYAN, the employee not only has the goal of customer satisfaction and loyalty in focus, but has a process whereby they can listen and interpret the potentially unique wants and needs of each customer in real time, and use the GYAN process to come up with the best possible customer outcome, every time.

Chapter Summary

Instead of a CRM system overlay, or the 'flavor of the month' customer initiative, GYAN can easily become a permanent part of your customer service culture. Since it is designed for the individual employee, it works for every employee in the entire organization, regardless of their title, experience level, or longevity.   And, it can work in every customer situation.

Use Situational Awareness and a dialogue with the customer to determine their expectations, and use the GYAN process to deliver. Now you know.

Chapter 8: GYAN Examples and Templates

The GYAN process is useful in service recovery situations, but it isn't limited to handling complaints. Here's an example of how GYAN can be applied to 'suggestive selling.'

Food servers know that if they can, through suggestive selling, they should try to increase the customer's order. The check total will increase, and their gratuity will probably increase, while the customer's dining experience will likely be enhanced.

Take the specific example of dessert. Employees at their pre-shift meeting are sometimes offered sample tastings, and reminded to 'push' dessert. That's the leadership that most server staff receive. But what happens if employees are aware of the GYAN process and its 10-point scale, and use it, the situation, and their own creativity to choose the customer experience numerical level they wish to achieve? Well, let's try putting the concept of selling dessert on the GYAN scale and have some fun with it.

As is the case with any customer/employee interaction, the food server has a full palette of phrases to use at the end of the meal concerning dessert. Think of what you could possibly say, in terms of a scale of 1 to 10, where: 1 discourages, a 5 is neutral, and 10 is the epitome of creative suggestive selling.

Here's an example of how GYAN might work with dessert. Using the GYAN scale of 1 to 10 for selling desert to customers that finished their main course, start by imagining what a '5' would be. Come up with a relatively neutral phrase, like: "Would you like some dessert?" Consider that statement a '5.' Now, in a training/mentoring environment, challenge your staff to try to come up with server statements to customers that would be below and above a '5' response.

Here goes: Your customers have just finished their meal and after clearing away dinner dishes and before you finalize their check, you'd like them to consider having dessert. So, you say, in a questioning tone: "Dessert?" It's probably not the best choice, but it happens a lot. But it's not the worst. It's probably a 3 or 4. The server could have chosen to say: "you don't want dessert, do you?" which is probably a 2 or 3. But how about: "from the looks of your waist-line, you don't need any more desserts, or anything else to eat for that matter." There's your zero.

Of course, no one would say that to a customer, but by using the GYAN scale, it teaches team members to use and expand their creativity and imagination, by being aware of the situation, and thinking. Thinking about alternatives, not just passively interacting verbally and responding robotically.

So, if "would you like some dessert?" is the 5, next you can work with your staff to coach them on the 'above 5' responses. Consider: "We have some excellent desserts... here's the menu" could be a 6. "You have to try our excellent desserts" might rate a 7. "My recommendation for an amazing dessert selection this evening is the chocolate mousse," could be an 8. What if you brought out the dessert tray and enthusiastically explained and raved about each one. That might qualify as a 9. And, a 10 might be: "we have the best desserts in town, and my personal favorite is the apple pie with vanilla ice cream." Or, another 10 might be: "The chef has prepared some excellent Crème Brule this evening. She let us sample it, and it's truly outstanding..." Or, "I like the Tiramisu, it's made here fresh, and I'll have the chef prepare it especially for you."

You get the idea. The GYAN Scale helps with awareness. But an awareness of, not just the words you're using, but the message you're sending, while allowing you to estimate how it will be received. This can make the difference between a good customer experience and a great one. We all have witnessed great employees that have a talent for providing superior customer service, no matter what the situation. But for those of us that are still developing that talent, the GYAN scale can be used by those that would like a tool to help them provide improved customer service and create better customer outcomes, within their own customer interactions.

GYAN Quiz

A Half-Eaten Chocolate Cake from Costco.

Situation: A customer purchased a cake last week. They bring it back to you today, half-eaten, with their receipt for proof of purchase in hand, explaining it didn't taste like chocolate cake. Use this example to determine how you should respond to this customer situation, using the GYAN process. For the purposes of this example, assume:

- A '5' would represent a response from you that would be perceived by the customer as average, typical or customer neutral.
- A '1' would represent a response from you that would create in the customer's mind, the least satisfactory feeling from their perspective.
- A '10' would represent a response from you that would create in the customer's mind, the most satisfactory customer outcome from their perspective.

If you were the employee facing the customer in this situation, what would you do? Based on a GYAN scale of 1-10 and the Costco information above, please complete the following, by indicating:

Your '5' Response:

_____

_____

_____

Your '1' Response:

_____

_____

_____

Your '10' Response:

_____

_____

_____

The Reason behind your Responses:

_____

_____

_____

'Spoiler Alert:' What did Costco do?

Gave the woman a sincere apology and a full cash refund, thanked her for sharing her experience, and invited her to try their other fresh baked goods.

Real-World GYAN Situations

Standardized response training, when dealing with unique individuals and circumstances, seldom leads to optimal customer satisfaction outcomes. But it's easier to train the staff to memorize greetings, than it is to figure out how to make every individual customer feel truly welcome. Here are a few sample situations where using GYAN during customer training can help managers improve customer outcomes, without creating scripted dialogues.

Standardized Greetings or Sincere Welcome? I recently dined in a relatively upscale chain restaurant. I was pleasantly greeted by 'Stephanie' who then asked if I had dined there before. I said yes, and she said: 'Well, welcome back.' In the absence of a more customer aware training environment, this consistency of greeting, ends up becoming what every employee must now routinely/robotically say each time. It becomes the standard. With the best of intentions, management attempts to simplify customer training by standardizing greetings to avoid greeting variances from one employee to another. While it accomplishes that, the problem is, that since it's a requirement to say it each time, it becomes routine, and loses its sincerity the more it's repeated. Customers soon recognize it's just something the employee was told to say each time, and the welcome feeling and recognition the restaurant tried to create, gets replaced with an artificial and forced conversation. Besides, my reservation and dining history was in their database, so they would have known, if they had done their homework. But even without checking, if 'welcome back,' is a 5, 'we're so happy to have you back with us,' might be a 6. Or, to get to an 8 or 9, ask the customer how their previous experience was, and then show your genuine commitment that no matter how good (or bad) the last visit was, this one is going to be the best ever.

I have found, that when you not only set outcome goals, but then give staff members the training tools and a little flexibility, they quickly 'get it' and end up happier in their job, while being surrounded every day by happier customers. Here are some additional GYAN process examples:

I'm Just Following the SOP-Orlando Hotel Lounge: Cocktail server smiles and says, "What can I get you?" After briefly discussing the GYAN process, I told the server that her greeting was a '5'. She justified it by saying it was part of the hotel's Standard Operating Procedures. I told her that she could increase her pay, if she followed a simple concept, and briefly discussed the Give Yourself A Number (GYAN scale of 1-10)." She thought for a brief moment, and then told me about the tropical drink specials, and how I could have their special Fiesta Margarita in a free Disneyworld souvenir glass. She got the GYAN process right away.

Last Minute Hotel Reservation: What customers want (VIPs and one-time walk-ins alike) is when they make a request, that it is at least acknowledged, and if you can't meet their request, try to meet their expectations in other ways. Customers know that their requests won't always be able to be met, like a couple requesting an upgrade to a deluxe Spa room, especially if they arrived at the last minute without making a reservation. So, as an employee using the GYAN process, your challenge is, when you receive a request for a specific 'something' (fill in the blank) and you don't have that specific thing, how can the GYAN process help?

Using the GYAN scale, first determine what a '5' response from you would be, given the type of request being made. A '5' response, when there are no deluxe spa rooms available, might be an acknowledgement of the request, and an apology. A '10' in this situation might be an upgraded room with a view, a small dish of chocolate covered strawberries for the couple to share, along with something to acknowledge the request (a 30 second hand-written note from you), and an apology for not being able to fulfill their request this time. (Yes, a note of apology, even if it's the customer's fault for not making an advance reservation). You could also offer a one-day guest pass to the hotel's private health club or an invitation to enjoy the spa at the pool.

Begging for Customer Satisfaction Ratings

During a recent business trip, I was sitting in a Florida hotel room, reading a form letter from the General Manager, wishing me a pleasant stay, and asking me to notify him, if I can't give him an 'Excellent' customer satisfaction rating on the customer survey card in the room's stationery folder when I leave. Begging customers for comment survey ratings is a way, but it's after the fact, and shows how little the unit manager knows about being proactively engaged and accessible to the customer at all times.

As mentioned previously, customer satisfaction involves satisfaction with the foundational aspects of the product or service (clean, functional, and meets basic needs). But customer satisfaction also involves how one feels about the experience. It isn't always the case that something is broken or missing and the customer wants it fixed or replaced. That's where GYAN can help. How? Because as your customer contact personnel are trained to be aware of not just what they will say in any given situation, but how their communication will be received, they will explore the various options they have at their disposal, that will help them deliver the best customer experience.

"I'm the Manager and you're not"

I've worked with hundreds of managers and thousands of supervisors, and those that delegate authority tend to be the most effective. Those that don't, tend to minimize the importance of empowering the customer contact employees, not taking advantage of the fact that the majority of issues could be handled without their involvement. For one thing, managers/supervisors are not always available, and for another, by delegating responsibility and authority, they can free up their time to contribute to the more strategic issues their organization faces.

Here's a simple but actual restaurant example involving breakfast item substitutions:

Guest: Can I substitute avocado for bacon in the breakfast burrito?
Server: No.
Guest: Do you have avocado?
Server: Yes, but we can't substitute it.
Guest: Can you check with your manager?
Server: (after checking, returned to table). Yes, it can be substituted.

I later met the manager to ask why it was necessary for the server to check with their supervisor, in order to satisfy a customer. He said they get all kinds of strange requests from customers, and to control costs, he doesn't want the servers to make the decision. I asked him if avocado was more expensive than bacon, and he said probably not. So, when I asked him why he couldn't just empower the employee, he shrugged his shoulders.[67] (As an aside, during our discussion, he said they used to have three restaurants, but now this is the only remaining location. Update: This location closed in 2014).

I stayed at a hotel near the Orlando Convention Center and had ordered room service the previous day. The following day, I received a call from a supervisor that the server failed to get my signature yesterday, and would I mind if they came up and got my signature now? When the server arrived, there were four water bottles in an ice bucket, along with an apology, and a friendly smile as he exited and thanked me for my business.

Compare that with a letter from the City of Los Angeles Revenue Dept., written to the owner of a small business, which said that a recent cross-check of other government records, indicated that the owner *may* not have a business license, and *may* owe additional taxes. When they went down to the local city office, showed their current license, and asked why they couldn't check their internal records first, before sending out the 'may' letter, the representative just said, they send out 'a lot of letters.'

I would invite you, when you are in the next situation where you are the customer, to evaluate your interaction using the GYAN process, and challenge yourself to come up with possible 1, 5, and 10 level responses that you could receive, given your situation. Then compare your results to what actually happens.

GYAN Examples

Here are some examples of situations and possible 'Give Yourself A Number' responses:

Restaurant: Customer: "Is it possible to have this left-over portion of my meal, prepared 'to go'?

1. Server says as she points: "Our 'to go' containers and other items are over there at the 'to go' counter."
5. Brings a Styrofoam container to your table and drops it off.
10. Removes your plate to the kitchen, attractively arranges your left-over meal in a container, adds fruit or a garnish, bags it, and hands it to you while thanking you for your business.

Bank: Customer: "I'd like to open an account."

1. "If you don't have an excellent credit score, it will be a waste of your time and mine."
5. "Great, start out by filling out these forms on the clipboard."
10. "You will love being part of our banking family. You will always have a great banking experience, because I will always be available to you as your personal banker, to make sure all your banking needs are met. We treat you like it's your money… because we understand that it is."

Meeting/exceeding expectations is one of the goals of using the GYAN process. But, you can also use GYAN yourself to help set expectations.

In Chapter 3: Delivering Customer Satisfaction, we talked about 'managing expectations,' and how doing so can improve customer satisfaction. The GYAN process is ideally suited for customer challenges like this. Take for example: business responsiveness. If you ask 100 people what they expect from a company they do business with, high on the list will be, 'I want them to be responsive.'

Business Responsiveness Example Using GYAN:
Customer: "I'd like to know when you will be done with the repairs."

 1. "I'll get back to you as soon as possible."
 5. "We're working on it right now."
10. "It will be done within 48 hrs."

Why don't people give you a specific time? As we discussed earlier in the book, some people find it easier to be vague like #1, or give a non-answer, like #5. That's because they would actually have to make a commitment to the customer, and to be able to do that, they would have to be organized and actually get back to the customer within 48 hours.

They probably feel they can't or don't want to, so they provide a good sounding but non-answer, with a number 5 reply. Instead, make a commitment, like in the number 10 reply. Provide your best estimate, and commit to it. If you run into something unexpected, and need some extra time, follow-up with the customer immediately, and discuss options, get further input from the customer, and make a new commitment.

GYAN can also be used to assess company culture.

How Managers View Employees Using GYAN:
Supervisors were asked for their perspective on employees that were their direct reports:

 1. "I have several employees working for me"
 5. "I work with…"
10. "I rely on my team. They're the ones interacting with the customer every day, and my job is to support them and help them do their best."

GYAN Exercises

Exercise 1: Here are several '5' responses. Use the GYAN process to come up with examples below (1-4) and above (6-10) and discuss.

Examples of situational phrases using the GYAN process that might be rated a '5.'
- I like your shoes
- The weather is fine
- It's good to hear from you
- You look nice today
- I'm feeling okay
- Nice job on that assignment
- All agents are busy, please hold
- You owe a balance of…
- After you request a menu item, server states we're out of that, and pauses

Exercise 2: Understanding the power of words using the GYAN Process.

Explain the difference between:
- 'I agree' compared to 'you are right'
- 'I can't schedule you for…, vs. 'I do have an appointment available on…, would that work?'
- 'You don't understand' vs. 'I didn't make myself clear.'
- 'I'll get back to you 'as soon as possible' vs. 'I'll get back to you within 24 hours, and if I need more time, I'll let you know in advance, where I am with the project.

Exercise 3: "Put it on the GYAN Scale" of 1 to 10.

Consider using the following next time you're training/mentoring your staff: Create a customer scenario, and using a real customer situation/comment (or make one up), ask for a suggested response to the customer request. Assign it a GYAN number from 1-10. Then, using the GYAN template, ask the group to come up with responses above and below the number assigned.

GYAN Training

The GYAN process can be incorporated as part of your current customer focused training. Whether you use internal human resources training/presentation modules, manuals/workbook handouts or online training services, the GYAN process can be easily incorporated into your customer training sessions. Some will wish to include it as part of their current training material and customize it to their particular needs. The GYAN template in the Appendix can serve as a starting point. Others may wish to use it as a separate module, to augment formalized internally developed or existing 3rd party customer training programs.

Since it's activity oriented, role-playing is a great way to effectively implement the GYAN process. Just include some training time that allows employees to learn and interact in a group setting. Volunteers can take turns giving examples and explaining how they will incorporate these customer focused lessons into their behavior in the future, when interacting with actual customers. One particularly useful training exercise is where employees take turns describing common customer situations they face, as the group decides the best response to create the highest value response. Session leaders can start the process by providing a '5' response, and then challenge the group to come up with '6' or '4' responses to the customer and go from there.

The goal is to engage the employee, in thinking through exercises that represent potential actual situations they might encounter, and to demonstrate the best way to respond. Session leaders monitor progress, answer questions, and fine-tune activities, while repeating, reinforcing and summarizing the key learning points, as everyone thinks of ways to use it in their customer contact situations. Here's an ancillary benefit to using the GYAN process: During a training session, invite the manager to drop in as an observer. They can see first-hand the challenges their front-line team face. As a result, they may want to implement changes to further improve employee empowerment and the customer service culture they create for their employees.

Can Customers use the GYAN Process?

They already are. Typically, as a customer approaches an employee with their issue, they are considering possible responses they might receive. If they are aware of the GYAN process, they can rank these anticipated responses from the best, to the response that would cause them to re-think remaining your customer, which helps them decide what an acceptable resolution might be from their perspective. One of the advantages of the GYAN Process, is that it can be used to estimate and quantify things that are generally viewed as not quantifiable, like feelings, emotions, and situational expectations, and therefore, can be used by employees as well as customers to come to the best customer outcome.

Here's an example of an employee's responses being evaluated using excerpts, taken from a book review post on Amazon.com concerning the book: *Customer Satisfaction is Worthless, Customer Loyalty is Priceless, by* well-respected author Jeffery Gitomer:[68]

"He [Gitomer] is not your rah-rah guy. Rather he's in your face, telling you how stupid it is to do some things, telling you how stupid it is NOT to do other things and always telling you… [to provide value]." And, "…to use your brain so you can be CREATIVE. Gitomer has fun and expects those who serve customers to have fun, too." Here's the example cited. "He talks about how he's greeted at the numerous hotels he checks into each year. Normally, it goes something like this, 'Checking in?' (To which the bald Gitomer is tempted to respond, 'NO, I'm here for my hair transplant'). He appropriately argues that the front desk receptionist could just as easily say, 'You look like you could use a nice, comfortable room. We've been waiting for your arrival. Welcome!' How much more effort would that take, argues Gitomer? None, it just takes a little bit of creativity and paying attention."

Was the front desk employee in the above example being rude? Not trained? Doesn't care? I don't think any of these things are true. I just think that to further improve customer loyalty, there needs to be a self-realization of what the employee is saying and then 'thinking' about *the way their message will be received* by the guest, before they say it. Then, it's a simple matter for the employee to decide what satisfaction level they want to 'create,' picking a greeting that will do that, and then say and do it. The GYAN process can help this front desk receptionist in the Jeff

Gitomer example, or any employee in any customer interaction, improve their customer's satisfaction and loyalty. How? By creating an awareness of the options that are available, and choosing the one that has the highest positive impact on customer loyalty.

What can be learned from the GYAN process in the context of the Gitomer example?

The front desk employee by just saying 'checking in?' is probably robotically repeating a phrase they have said hundreds of times. But more importantly, the awareness level of how their words *will be received* is low. And, they do not see the huge opportunity they have to help elevate the arriving customer's initial perception of the hotel and the arrival experience. The power of the GYAN process, is that a brief, five-minute discussion about the concept with that front desk staff member, would not only increase their awareness level, but the customer service they provide would also increase in concrete ways, as the way they greet arriving customers from now on, could forever change for the better.

But perhaps more importantly, the GYAN process was already embedded within the arriving customer. Maybe not formally, but it's not difficult to use the GYAN Process to help demonstrate, that the usually nebulous things like 'expectations' can be quantified. When the front desk employee asked if he was 'checking in?' you could assign a number, say a 5, to the greeting that he received. It's clear that the arriving customer had an expectation of a response that would be higher on the GYAN scale. So, while an accusatory statement like the one given might rate a 5, a greeting offering some sort of a 'welcome' would rate a 7 or 8, and help get their visit off to a great start. And, for the customer, a service level at or higher than expected, often leads to a more positive customer experience, and ultimately, Customer Loyalty.

Chapter Summary
Incorporating the GYAN process into your current customer service training, will not only be fun and engaging for your staff, but help them understand that customer interactions can actually be successfully managed. And with practice, it will not only help improve customer loyalty, but make their interactions with customers more interesting and rewarding for the employee as well.

Chapter 9: GYAN Implementation

Situational Awareness & Reasoned Empowerment

People have told me that the GYAN process has permanently changed the way they look at customer interactions. Not just when they're helping customers, but also when they themselves are the customer.

And, once you are aware of the 'Give Yourself A Number' process and how it works, you can begin using it right away. But to make it work most effectively and consistently in a business environment, two critical aspects must be in place for every customer contact employee: Situational Awareness and Reasoned Empowerment.

Situational Awareness: It involves assessment of the current customer situation, deciding on what type of customer experience you are going to create, and finally, an awareness of the likelihood of what you plan on doing will achieve the right customer outcome.

In every employee/customer interaction, after the employee listens to the customer, they need to think about and decide what they plan to say to the customer. But by using the GYAN process, before responding, the employee goes through a second thought process. They need to anticipate/estimate how the customer will likely react to what they are planning to say next, based on what outcome the employee would like to accomplish. This goal is usually a highly satisfied, more loyal customer, but it could be any targeted outcome. Then, before saying anything, give what they are planning on telling the customer a score from 1 to 10 of how likely 'what they are planning to say' will be to getting their desired response/outcome from the customer.

The employee is thinking through the situation, not just about what they may have said in the past, but based on the employee's assessment of this unique customer standing in front of them, and the current situation thus far, self-grading what they are about to say, in terms of how it will be *received* by the customer. This additional step in the typical customer/employee interaction allows the employee to measure/self-assess the effectiveness of what they will be saying in terms of accomplishing the desired customer outcome.

As we've discussed, the real 'value added' customer solution is not always apparent, at least initially. The best solutions take into account the uniqueness of the customer and an assessment of the current situation. Further, it may not even be what the employee's first thought is, or even what the customer is requesting. But when you take the time to focus, not on just your actions, but how likely those actions will accomplish the outcome you desire, you are in a better position to come up with an optimal solution.

This deeper awareness of customer interaction is helpful in several ways. Instead of the employee's robotic response, even typically good robotic responses, are now being evaluated by the employee, before anything is said to the customer. This gives the employee the opportunity to tailor their statement to the situation at hand, and thereby deliver a 'customized' response, allowing the employee to respond in a contemplative way rather than just react, and that's when personal creativity gets a chance to work. This increases the probability of an improved and personalized customer experience, which is the key to taking your customer loyalty process to the next level.

It also leads to enhanced job satisfaction, not just in the improved customer outcomes, but in the interesting and challenging solutions that the customer service employee creates, versus repetitive mundane scripted responses repeated over and over again.

Martin Buber, 20th century theologian (1878-1965), discussing modes of existence and interactions in which individuals engage with other individuals, told a story that changed his life. When he was young, his parents were divorced and he went to live on his grandparent's farm. He would feed the animals, clean the pens, and groom the horses. One day, when Buber was about eleven, he was caring for a horse which was his particular favorite. He loved to ride and groom and feed that horse, and often brought it special treats, and the horse seemed to respond and liked the boy who fed and combed it so well. As Buber was stroking the horse's neck one day, a strange feeling came over him. He felt that he could not only understand what it felt like to be an eleven-year-old boy patting a horse, but he could understand what it must have felt like to be a horse being patted by a boy. The joy of that moment, of being able to go beyond the confines of his own soul and know what another soul was experiencing, led him to create an entire theology on that feeling.[69]

Customer relations is just that: a relationship. A relationship where both sides are continuously evaluating how they are being treated by the other in the relationship, and responding (making the relationship better/stronger or worse/weaker) depending on how they perceive they are being treated. In other words, is the person on the other side, adding value/happiness, or subtracting? By the employee directionally 'experiencing' the other side of the relationship before saying or doing anything, the GYAN process helps to improve the chances that the customer experience will be better, and the customer relationship will be stronger.

Reasoned Empowerment: In addition to Situational Awareness, the second critical factor that must be present for the GYAN process to work effectively, is employee empowerment. Reasoned employee empowerment is required to allow the employee to have the authority, to not only customize their response, but to maximize the customer's satisfaction and achieve the desired customer outcome during the initial contact.

What we're discussing with the GYAN process is a measurement taken in real-time and ideally, at multiple times over the complete pre-purchase, purchase, and post-purchase relationship. This linking of the GYAN process, with the real-time customer relationship and your product/services, gives you plenty of time to control the outcome, and if something goes wrong, correct the situation. This is where Reasoned Empowerment comes in. Reasoned, because even if you have all the authority in the world, you still need to make a value judgment about how far you will go to maximize the customer's experience. (Usually the cost of the remedy weighed against the potential life-time value of the customer).

The point is, that authority to make corrections, (like refunds, or similar steps that might negatively impact short-term financial results) is not limitless, and it shouldn't be. But if your employees are not empowered now, and you need a cadre of supervisors to make routine approval authorizations, you're overstaffed, wasting time, and reducing the job satisfaction of front-line employees who have to check with someone every time a customer needs something.

How much authority to delegate? You should delegate enough authority so that as a rule of thumb, 90% or more of the decisions that need to be made can be made without the initial customer contact employee needing to contact anyone else for additional authority. (Note to supervisors: As customer contact employees come to you with issues needing authority beyond theirs, after you give your guidance, do your own assessment of the issue. Ask yourself: "Was this something that should be resolved in the future by delegating additional authority to your front-line staff?" If your sole function is granting approvals, start looking for other ways to add organizational value (or stroke your ego), before *your* supervisor finishes reading this book).

The concept outlined in the Give Yourself A Number (GYAN) process is easily grasped at all levels of the organization and at its core, the framework of the process is simple. It can even be summarized on a single page, (see page 137). But it's based on the understanding of the complex set of interactions, thought processes, directional interactions and even emotions, that can potentially take place in everyday customer interactions, and establishes a process that is not only easily understood, but actionable as well. It's also interesting and mentally challenging, as employees use their creativity, experience, and knowledge to come up with unique solutions to the situations they face.

And the GYAN process doesn't just improve your customer scores and customer loyalty. It also has a positive effect on morale. Armed with the tools and perspective of the GYAN process, customer interactions are positive experiences for employees as well. Problems can occur in even the best run organizations. Employees have told me that they enjoy the mental challenge of solving problems instead of just apologizing for them. They have said that they have a renewed sense of confidence, a 'can do' mentality in dealing with customers and in other aspects of their life. They enjoy using the GYAN process to think through situations, and come up with an estimated 'best' solution, for real-life situations and circumstances that they face every day. Use the GYAN process and you will start seeing positive changes in behaviors at all levels of the organization. And, as skills are developed that allows the GYAN process to be used proactively, your staff will evolve, from 'correcting problems' to 'anticipating needs.' It becomes a win/win for everyone involved, including you.

Can Success be just a 'Perspective'

How you mentally approach customer service goes a long way in determining how successful you will be at it. For example, ask yourself the question, 'Does it matter if you are problem oriented or solution oriented?' In my experience, how you look at any situation will help determine its outcome. It's your mindset and your perspective that counts.

Take a customer complaint as an example. You can either look at the situation as, 'This customer is giving me their complaint' (problem oriented), or 'I will find a way to resolve the customer's issue' (solution oriented). Or take empowerment for example. Ask yourself as an employee, is 'empowerment' something a supervisor gives to me, or is it something that gives me an opportunity to create?

The GYAN process is about changing perspectives. Most employees in customer service situations, focus on what they are going to say or do. GYAN has taught us it's not about the message you send, it's about how the message you send, is received.

According to Don Peppers and Martha Rogers, Ph.D. in *Rules to Break and Laws to Follow,* to create a superior customer experience requires understanding the customer's point of view. "What is it really like to be your customer? What are the day-in, day-out customer experiences your company is delivering? How does it feel to wait on hold on the phone? To open a package and not be certain how to follow the poorly translated instructions? To stand in line, be charged a fee, to wait for a service call that was promised two hours ago, to come back to an online shopping cart that's no longer there an hour later? Or what's it like to be remembered? To receive helpful suggestions? To get everything exactly as it was promised? To be confident that the answers you get are the best ones for you?" (Peppers and Rogers 2008).[70]

So far in this chapter, we've discussed situational awareness and reasoned empowerment. They are both vital to reaching the full potential value of the GYAN process. They help the employee use the situation, empowerment, and their creativity and people skills, to come up with the highest possible customer outcome. And if success is a mindset, it's the perspective you have when faced with a customer problem, that will help determine if it gets resolved to the customer's satisfaction, or not.   It's also a personal commitment to accept responsibility for the outcome.   But what if the solution that you've offered, hasn't satisfied the customer?   If that's true, then in the above situation, you haven't satisfied the customer, 'yet.'

The Power of the Word 'Yet'

This change of perspective, from 'problem oriented' to 'solution oriented' service delivery can be assisted by the concept I refer to as: '*The Power of Yet*'.

I experienced it first hand while at Hilton Hotels Corporation.   During a school career day that Hilton sponsored for students at a local middle school, I had the chance to discuss career goals with four students, including a 10-year-old student named Maria, who wanted to become a nurse.   I asked her what was her favorite subject in school and she said she liked everything but math.   When asked why, she said she wasn't good at it.   After convincing her of the importance of a nurse knowing math, (measuring vital signs, computing medication dosage, etc.), I suggested to her that she wasn't good at math 'yet.'   She thought for a moment, and then I asked her if she was 'good at math.'   She paused, smiled, and then instead of saying no, she said: "Not *Yet*."

Every thought you have sends a message through your body that either strengthens you or weakens you.   These thoughts create impressions in the mind, good or bad, conscious or unconscious.   And as the young student provided answers to the questions about her future aspirations, and the things she either hasn't done, or has tried and failed, I suggested she just add to her thought process, the phrase: 'not yet.'

You see, in my experience, if you tell yourself you can't do something, you end up being correct.   You are not good at it, because you tell yourself you're not.   You minimize your potential yourself, as you don't start doing the things that could make you succeed.   Once you say, 'not yet' you are now making a choice; of whether or not to spend the time studying, practicing, rehearsing to accomplish something, or postponing/avoiding action that could help you.   So, if you're not good at something that you want to learn or accomplish, just change the internal message you send, and add 'not yet.'   Then, you start thinking, if I study hard, I can learn it, and when I decide to practice hard I will accomplish it. And pretty soon, the sky is not the limit and you can do anything you set your mind to, including satisfying the most difficult and challenging issues you may face.

<u>Chapter Summary</u>
Just being intimately aware of the decision-making situation you are in and being empowered, will help make the GYAN process work for your organization, its customers, and you. Challenge yourself to creatively work to provide the solutions with the highest customer value outcome.

Look at problems, not as problems, but as situations that need solutions. And finally, by adding this simple GYAN module to your training program, shown on the next page, it will not only improve customer satisfaction and loyalty, but improve employee morale as well.

GYAN: Simple 5 Step Training Outline

After greeting the customer, evaluate & understand the situation you are in. If it involves a customer request:

1. Listen/Assess: **Listen** carefully to the customer (paying attention to verbal as well as non-verbal communications) so you can **Assess** and understand the customer's issue.

2. Plan/Think: Then, with the **Plan** of exceeding the customer's expectations in mind, **Think** about the options you have and what you might say or do, to reach the intended customer outcome.

3. Quantify/Evaluate: **Quantify** the options you have, by creating and ranking the possible things you might say or do on a scale of 1 to 10. Then, pick one. But before responding to the customer, **Evaluate** your choice by estimating on a scale of 1 to 10, how likely what you're planning to say or do will be, in achieving the desired positive customer outcome. (From 1=very unlikely, to 10=very likely). Keeping in mind your goal is to provide a solution to the customer request, while increasing customer loyalty.

4. Respond: Based on the number grade you gave yourself, if you're satisfied with what you are about to say (i.e., a score of 8 or higher), **Respond** by saying it to the customer. If not, think of a response that you can give, that would result in a higher number, and say that instead. (This is the time for the employee to use their imagination, insight, training, experience and customer focused talent they have, to come up with an 8 or higher response, and then respond to the customer).

5. Observe/Act, or Reassess: **Observe** the customer's reaction. If you feel the customer's reaction was an 8, 9 or 10, then **Act**. Do what you said you would do. If the customer's reaction is 7 or less, **Reassess.** Think through the situation again, using the customer's reaction and their comments as additional input. Use your skills, personality, training, experience and imagination, and come up with something else better to say/do, as you repeat step 3 above.

Continue the process, until you're satisfied that you've achieved the highest possible customer outcome.

Chapter 10: When Things Go Wrong: Service Recovery

"Customers don't expect you to be perfect. They do expect you to fix things when they go wrong." - Donald Porter V.P., British Airways

Who is Responsible for Customer Service Recovery?

Back in Part I of the book, when talking about customer satisfaction, we asked the question, 'Who is responsible for delivering customer service?' The answer, in general, was that providing customer service is everyone's job. But what about when things go wrong? Is the answer different? Who is responsible for customer service *recovery*? When it comes to service recovery, (or complaint handling or problem resolution), the reality is that most companies and websites have dedicated customer service departments to handle them. The idea is that these centralized groups of customer service representatives (phone, mail, email, chat, or in-store customer service departments), not only handle general questions, but are specifically trained and skilled in the art of customer service recovery.

But companies have long struggled with the concept of dedicated customer service employees and the challenges of operating those so called 'customer service' departments/centers. Take Delta Airlines for example. According to *USA Today*,[71] back in the 1960s Delta pioneered the concept of 'Red Coats.' These were 'out front' highly visible customer service representatives whose job was to provide information and assistance in the event a customer had a question or problem. Then, for budgetary reasons, they disappeared. After having one of the worst consumer complaint records in the industry, Delta recently brought them back, saying in their blog: "Our Red Coat agents are selected and trained with exceptional technical and customer service skills to provide on-the-spot resolution of customer issues.'[72] Taking a different approach, British Airways has a program called First-request service. Their guidelines say that: "A customer should only have to contact a business once to have his or her problem solved or question answered." So which approach is correct? Should you have dedicated customer service representatives or not?

Like anything in life, it depends. Depending on the type of product or service you offer, you may need to provide an easy way to reach a customer service team, just to give the customer easy access to product/service questions, refunds/exchanges or technical support. But if the customer has a complaint and if you don't train/empower your front line/first contact employees in problem resolution, customer service centers, like outsourced call centers, can become complaint dumping grounds. And, if all your front line/first contact employees are available, trained, and empowered, a separate, dedicated customer service group may not be needed. Each company needs to decide what customer experience/customer recovery result they want to achieve, and create an organization structure that gets their desired end result.

Having said that, my vote in general, is to not have a separate group. A dedicated customer service team, with their mission statement to: 'focus on the customer,' may sound like a good idea, but only if you've given up on the idea of having customer satisfaction on everyone's position description. You see, it's far too easy to delegate the customer satisfaction job to the person in the red coat, then it is for everyone to take responsibility for the customer's satisfaction and fixing system-wide customer issues in the first place. And, from the customer's perspective, they mentioned the issue to you, and then you referred them to the 'customer service team.' So, even if ultimately the issue gets resolved, the story often had to be told two (or more) times. If you haven't developed a culture where customer satisfaction is everyone's job (and trained, empowered, and allowed them to take ownership of solving the customer's issue), then maybe a dedicate customer service department is the way to go. But only until you've figured out how to make it everyone's job, or you've dressed everyone in the company, including the CEO, in red.

Let's take a look at what happens when things go wrong, and try to analyze what occurs when a customer complains.

Anatomy of a Customer Complaint

Most companies understand that customer loyalty is vital to their success, so they work very hard to prevent customer problems and complaints. No one wants to hear that a customer is unhappy... not the business owner, not the manager and especially not the employee standing in front of the person with the complaint. But while everything is done to avoid a complaint, they are something that every organization eventually faces.

In general, there are three component parts that make up most complaints, and they all follow a similar pattern:

  1: The Communication: Customer describes complaint
  2: The Dialogue between the employee and the customer
  3: The Conclusion/Resolution

<u>1: The Communication: Customer describes the actual complaint.</u> The typical complaint involves a communication (text, voice or in person) from the customer with the complaint to the employee/service provider. The customer states the issue and the employee receives the complaint. As the parties interact, the specifics of the complaint are made known. It can involve the service level received, the product, or a whole host of problems that the customer feels have occurred. The thing you can say in general, is that customer expectations were not met.

<u>2: The Dialogue.</u>   In most employee/customer interactions, the interchange takes the form of an iterative two-way communication. In the case of an in-person complaint: one speaks while the other person listens. Then they respond, while the original speaker listens. Customer (A) speaks to Employee (B) as B listens. Then B responds to what A said, as A listens, and so it goes.

The dialogue starts when the employee reacts to the initial complaint. Once the employee knows that something is wrong, and after attentively listening and apologizing as they were trained, the employee begins a complex thought process to mentally search for possible customer solutions (the GYAN process is ideal for service recovery).   The employee then mentally overlays the proposed solution against what can be called their 'boundary of responses' (internal policies, procedures and past practices). From that, they determine a response that gets the highest customer anticipated outcome, within the constraints of their individual authority. The employee also reflects on their own personal experiences, and assesses the likelihood that their supervisor would be available and willing to enter the situation if necessary.

After the employee responds, the customer also goes through some mental self-searching. They may have anticipated resistance, and begin thinking of scenarios that, while less optimal, would still be an acceptable resolution. They also assess their 'leverage quotient,' (i.e., are they a recognized frequent customer, and/or do they have any power that they could exert to help them get the resolution they want)? For example, would the threat of a negative social media review give the customer additional leverage. Or, would saying that they will never purchase your products/services again, be enough of a threatened loss to give them leverage, or does the employee even care. Would they be able to speak to the manager? Then the emotional aspect can enter in. If they feel the employee is unwilling or unable to 'right a wrong,' they might escalate (for example, by changing their tone or raising voice) and become more demanding/threatening. And, if they feel that wouldn't help, they may reduce their expectations somewhat, and mentally review the possible lesser outcomes that would still be acceptable. So, the complaining customer reviews the 'offer' and compares the employee's response against their perceived wants and needs to determine if it satisfies them. If it does, it's accepted by the customer.

If the offer is not accepted, a message is sent back to the employee. The complaining customer will either raise the stakes, or offer some indication that they are willing to compromise. The employee will again mentally check for possible solutions based on the new feedback from the customer. If the employee can improve the 'offer' the message is sent back to the customer. If not, there is usually an additional apology and the customer's wants and needs remains potentially unsatisfied, and anxiety is heightened on both sides.

Resistance, anger, and escalation (bringing the issue to someone with more authority) can sometimes occur. The problem is either resolved at this next higher level or it remains unsatisfied.

3: The Conclusion/Resolution.   If accepted by the customer, the complaint is considered resolved. Just remember, that even though the complaint may be resolved, the way it was resolved can result in unchanged, enhanced, or diminished customer loyalty. Obviously, after exhausting all possibilities, if the customer is still not satisfied, the business and the customer then decide if the outcome of the situation will affect their future business relationship.

Lost Business-Avoiding Customer Churn

'Now that we have you, how do we keep you?'

Every day, someone makes the decision not to return as a customer, and most of the time no one notices. They just stop buying your product or services. It could have been caused by a problem that wasn't fixed, like a late shipment, a price/value issue, or a wrong order. It is generally a problem that was either not recognized or recognized and not fixed. The problem is you hear about customer 'churn' all the time, but human nature being what it is, you think it doesn't apply to your company or to the situation you're in now. In some companies, there's an acceptance that a certain amount of customer churn is natural and normal. This attitude seems okay until the numbers of lost customers becomes significant. By that time, it's generally too late to do anything about it.

It's like you are aware of it in the back of your mind, but don't make the connection that the situation you're in now, is one of those situations where you could lose a customer. And sometimes, even when they tell you they might leave as your customer, you might not believe them. So, even if you're not in denial, there must be a million reasons for customer churn/attrition, right? Actually, according to a recent study[73] there are only four.

> 68%: Leave because of the treatment they've received
> 14% Dissatisfied with product or service
> 9% Begin doing business with the competition
> 9% Seek alternatives, move away, die

Think about it: According to the above research if a customer has a complaint, how the customer feels they were treated during the complaint process is almost five times more important in keeping a customer, than the product or service you provided.

Here's the problem: Treating customers well is the goal of anyone and everyone who has customers. Yet when they're not treated properly, it's the main reason they stop supporting your organization. So, there must be a perception gap between the way organizations think they are treating their customers, and the way customers think they are being treated. And in this battle of perceptions, the customer always wins.

So, a good starting point in evaluating the problem of customer churn, is to ask yourself, "How am I treating my customers?" If you feel there's room for improvement, the next issue you face, is: "What am I going to do about it?"

But because of the potential different expectations and needs that each customer may have, along with the potential uniqueness of every situation, the old adage: "you can't satisfy all of the people all of the time," seems to be true. So, most aim for 'most of the people, most of the time.'

Wait. Let's stop for a second. If you hear someone say, 'oh well, you can't satisfy everyone', what are they really trying to communicate? In my experience, it's a statement usually used by someone to justify a failed customer service recovery interaction. This is the type of declarative statement that tries to deflect criticism, but it's more damaging than that. It avoids the thought and effort that could go into satisfying the unsatisfied customer that just left. Plain and simple, it's an excuse for not knowing, or knowing and not making the right customer decision.

Superior customer service, because it's delivered individually, is an individually developed talent. If the person in the next room has it, it doesn't help you. But there's hope. The GYAN process can help, but you need to understand it, practice using it, and go through the thought process and the hard work, to develop the talent. There's no shortcut to sincere and helpful customer service, every time, for every customer.

But the good news is, once you use the GYAN process and develop your talent for exceeding customer expectations, or resolving customer issues, you have it forever. GYAN can change your outlook and your perspective on dealing with problems, but not just customer problems, it can help you with the way you solve the everyday issues you face too.

Now, back to the question, "can you satisfy everyone, every time?" The answer is yes. GYAN helps your team go through the thought process of creatively looking for and finding solutions in even the most difficult situations. Now, the question is not, can you, but do you want to? This is much different. It's solution oriented instead of just giving excuses; and it's empowering. You work to find a solution, and then use business guidelines and your knowledge and your own talent to satisfy the customer issues.

Importance of Service Recovery

Service recovery is probably one of the most misunderstood topics in modern day customer management circles. It's amazing, but it's almost as if supervisors all over the U.S. have told customer contact employees that a complaining customer is either lying or out to get something for nothing, and you must resist giving it to them if you can.

So, what is service recovery? Actually, the goal is the same as when we talked about customer satisfaction and creating customer loyalty initially. It's just that instead of creating or maintaining satisfaction and loyalty, your goal is to repair it, and if possible, make it even better and stronger.

So, while in most customer/business interactions, problems are relatively rare, when they do occur, service recovery is an extremely important process. The reason: customers assign more weight to how well you resolve a problem than they do when things go well from the beginning. Complaint resolution also has more impact on customer loyalty, than just having a good, problem-free, overall customer experience. That's because a good experience is the 'norm.' It's what was anticipated in the first place and it's what the customer is paying for, so when it happens, it's no big deal, because it's expected.

But while meeting or exceeding customer expectations is the goal, sometimes things will go wrong. And when they do, your employees should think of one word: Opportunity. When a problem comes up, the goal of service recovery is not just problem resolution, but it's to maintain and even enhance customer loyalty. The 10% or so of problems a company experiences should get management's complete focus, so they can be properly resolved, because once a customer decides to defect, it takes more than just returning to the way things were, to get the customer's loyalty back.[74]

And if you look at complaints from the customer's perspective, they may be taking the time to complain because they are hoping that someone will listen, recognize their importance, and take some positive action. This scenario usually represents a customer who wants to be loyal and remain a customer, and will judge how well their complaint is handled, to decide.

<u>What about the number of complaints that an organization receives?</u>
The fewer the complaints, the higher the customer loyalty, right? Well, yes and no. Complaints are going to happen, even if it's a small number. Not everything is under your control, and customers can be unreasonable. And while it's true that a satisfied customer is more likely to return than one that has complained, it's only true if the complaint is not resolved properly. If someone told you that they have a low level of complaints, and to them, that indicates that their customers are loyal, what would you think? If only 4% of your customers complain, is that good? Are the other 96% satisfied? They may or may not be satisfied, but they are all at risk.

<u>What if a company already has a high level of complaints?</u>
Be careful in judging. They might be open and even encouraging customers with problems to share them, and take advantage of the 'opportunities' complaints offer. Organizations and employees in a customer focused environment may be viewed by their customers as welcoming feedback, good or bad. Further, if we develop and set targets for reducing the number of complaints, we might adversely affect internal behaviors by reducing our willingness to listen to customers. So, the better metric to measure is not complaints, but unresolved complaints.

Want another reason to embrace complaints? Most businesses try to discover problems and correct them so that the problem doesn't occur again, since they cost time, money and customer goodwill. But what if your company is not aware of an internal condition or procedural problem that is creating customer dissatisfaction and is recurring? And what if you could get someone to discover the problem for you, and tell you about it, and it wouldn't cost you anything to get the information? Sounds like a good deal, right? It's called a customer complaint.

Yet, for many businesses and their supervisors and employees, it's just the opposite. Instead of welcoming complaints so loyalty for that particular customer can be forever strengthened, complaints are looked upon as a nuisance to be avoided, or delegated to the newest, least experienced staff member to handle.

And when a complaint is not handled properly, not only is the customer relationship damaged, but the employee is negatively impacted as well. That's why employees that 'handle' complaints, like those that work in customer call centers or customer support teams, when not empowered to resolve customer issues, eventually feel a sense of burn-out.

Is there a better way to handle complaints, where it's more likely that a satisfactory solution will occur and loyalty maintained? That's where using the GYAN process can help to come up with quicker and better solutions.

Learning to resolve customer complaints is essential for any organization that has customers. GYAN allows employees to actually resolve issues, and in so doing, customers' satisfaction (and repeat business) not only goes up, but so does the sense of accomplishment for the employee who now experiences a positive customer/employee interaction.

But service recovery is more than simple empowerment, so you can give the customer what they want. It takes everyone working together towards the same goal and vision of the customer, to enable the customer to realize that wherever they are, and whoever they contact with their issues, it will get resolved to their satisfaction. This is where creating the right working culture throughout the organization is required. The goal is to create a network of customer focused employees, in different departments with different responsibilities but all on the same page, working as one to create and maintain Customer Loyalty. Implementing the GYAN process system-wide will help with your customer focused culture development efforts, since every employee that a customer comes in contact with, will have the tools they need. It's like learning a common customer service language throughout the organization. The entire staff will understand getting to the highest customer outcome is not only a goal, but it's achievable. Why is this network or customer culture important? It's not only so that anyone anywhere can provide customer assistance, but also, many times the solution requires 'cross-functional cooperation from or among other departments' to make the correction.[75]

When it comes to customer satisfaction, if employees in your organization don't feel a 'shared purpose' culture, or there isn't an interdepartment cooperative service recovery working environment, what happens? They might:

  a) Give an apology for not resolving the complaint, or
  b) say 'that's not my job.'

Both are easier than to accept responsibility for resolving a problem they didn't create, or trying to find a solution that they feel they don't have direct control over.

In the first case it really is easier to give an apology while saying no to the customer. You may not know what should be done, or view the solution as excessive so you don't try. In the second case, it may not be your job, if you look at your job as a narrowly focused departmental function, instead of your job being an integrated team of networked employees with different functional skill sets, but with a unity of purpose whose ultimate responsibility and shared vision, is to build customer loyalty. If you see increasing customer loyalty as your job, you take the time to develop your customer satisfaction skills, and you willingly (and gratefully) engage with the dissatisfied customer and work to develop a solution for any customer situation. Instead of just saying you are sorry over and over (talk about a demotivating job), use GYAN to resolve customer issues, and you'll feel a sense of pride and confidence as a result of your accomplishment, and build customer loyalty in the process. Finally, don't just handle customer complaints, embrace them.

Complaints are your Friend

"The complaining customer represents a huge opportunity for more business."
Zig Ziglar

It may seem counter-intuitive, but the very best opportunity to strengthen or rebuild customer loyalty, is when something goes wrong. That's why customer complaints are so important. It's not just to fix the issue the customer raised. They are communicating with you and that means you have an opportunity to increase/strengthen the loyalty bond.

As we mentioned earlier, to the unenlightened, customer complaints are unpleasant for the employee because most customer service interactions involve employees that are not empowered or not focused on the goal to increase customer loyalty. Their job is to *handle* the complaint. That usually involves an apology, or a refund, a repair/exchange, or some other one-dimensional resolution. For example, as a customer, has this ever happened to you? Something goes wrong and you bring it to an employee's attention. Their response: 'We are very sorry. It was an unfortunate error that doesn't happen very often, and it's not who we are. We will fix it so it won't happen again.'

First of all, how many times a complaint happens, is your organization's problem, not the customer's. And the fact that you say you will 'fix' it so it won't happen to some future customer is also meaningless. 'It happened to me, and you may have 'fixed' it for the future, but that didn't resolve it for me.' And, most people think when you fixed it, you're done. You're not done. Not until you've maintained or enhances the current customer's loyalty in the process.

How can the GYAN process be used when you receive a customer complaint? Simple. After the customer explains the situation, use GYAN, to develop a response. Just make sure that what you do next creates value for the customer in excess of the potential loss of goodwill. Because if the resolution is not accomplished in a timely manner, or if the customer has to use leverage or escalate and then gets resolution, the impact can still be negative and their loyalty diminished, even if the problem is resolved. The goal is to have the customer satisfied with immediate issues, while creating an expectation of a quick and easy resolution of a future problem, should one occur. This will lead to making the 'Loyalty Bond' even stronger than before the incident generating the complaint occurred.

Hopefully if you've read this far, no one equates satisfied customers with loyal ones, but as a business owner/manager, are you ready to take the next step? That is, to feel fortunate that you have complaints? Yes, I said fortunate. Instead of leaving and never returning, your customer has chosen to communicate their wants and needs to you, and to let you know that the product/service they received, didn't meet their expectations. Well, if they take the time to complain, they are voluntarily in direct communication with you. Though you probably received their feedback after the fact, you still have the opportunity to determine if their expectations were reasonable, and if they were, and you want to keep them as a customer, you can still work to recapture and even enhance their loyalty. And you can accomplish this. Just use their real-time customer input (their complaint) to exceed their expectations now.

My perspective is that customer complaints are a rich source of customer feedback that can help you provide better service, create loyalty, and grow market share. But what if 'culturally' that feedback opportunity isn't available. We know that customer service levels in Japan tend to be relatively high. And Japanese customers tend not to openly complain, even if they are not happy with the product or service. Given this tendency not to complain, my sense is that Japanese company/service providers are aware of this, and realize that they won't know as often when the customer feels there was a service breakdown. So, their unsatisfied customers become the proverbial customer that didn't complain, and just won't come back. There is also a high propensity to share experiences with others, good or bad. The implication is that with less actual customer feedback/information, organizations must 'over-anticipate' or 'guess-high' when determining what service level they must provide or what level of service recovery to use, that will result in a satisfied customer.

Complaints can give you another chance to keep a customer, and one more reason to be appreciative, when your customer shares their feedback, especially negative feedback with you.

As for the remaining 90+% customers that don't complain, there's a dichotomy between being thankful that they don't complain and being worried about them. If your customers aren't complaining, it could be good but it could be bad; you don't know for sure. They may be exceedingly loyal and happy, or they may have given up and left forever. One of the advantages of loyalty programs discussed in Chapter 4, is that they do provide a way to maintain ongoing communications with the customer. You can verify frequency of purchase, and the level and trend of spend, and offer incentives to generate more frequent purchases, or to re-start purchases. But even without a loyalty program, look for ways to communicate with your customers every chance you get.

Look for ways to get feedback, not just at the end of the transaction, when customers are presented with a bill or register receipt, but at any time, during the pre-purchase/purchase/post-purchase phases. Knowing how your customer perceives the service they are receiving in real time, gives you an opportunity to correct issues as they occur. And even if there isn't an issue, just having the manager stop by your restaurant table to say hello for example, creates recognition and customer empowerment.

We mentioned before a situation where, even though a customer was 100% satisfied, they thought they might be more satisfied somewhere else. Everything went well according to the satisfied guest, but they still weren't loyal.

So, when things go right, even consistently right, you still need to have some customer feedback/engagement mechanism to gauge whether or not the customer's expectations are shifting to a higher level. This could mean that today's level of satisfaction provided is good, but won't work tomorrow. So even if customers are completely satisfied now, if you're not communicating with them, they too are at risk.

Continuous Improvement

If you have a Continuous Improvement culture, creating a feedback link from those who receive and resolve customer complaints, will not only help you further improve the services you provide, but eliminate future problems from recurring.

Here's an example of what can happen when there's no feedback loop between those responsible for delivering customer service and those handling complaints.

When a duplicate medical services charge is received by a patient who paid for the services in advance, the resolution center assumes its job is done, when they research the issue, find the duplicate billing, and tell the customer the duplicate charge will be removed from their account at the end of the month. That's not it. An organization that was interested in continuously improving their services would have a process after it's resolved with the customer to have it investigated internally, and determine how to change the current process so it doesn't happen again. Managers and administrators often see payroll, supplies and objective costs as the thing to control, when the real cost saving issue in the example above, is reducing the indirect costs associated with the procedures that caused the incorrect billing, like staff time to review and correct the problem, the risk of it happening again for another patient, and the damage it does to the customer's impression of how the medical facility operates. After all, if they can't get a simple billing issue correct, what else could go wrong there?

Problems that you are not aware of occur all the time, and if you're not engaged in a dialogue with your customers 24/7, you may not realize anything is wrong. So, as much as you and your employees don't like hearing complaints, it is not only the single best opportunity to regain and increase customer loyalty, but you can use the feedback to constantly improve the services you provide. How?

Use a feedback loop from your customer service group to determine what customers are complaining about. Then, look into the root cause of problems, prioritizing issues that create customer complaints, and develop a plan to correct whatever went wrong, and communicate the new initiative or process internally. It means putting in place a process for continuous improvement.

Continuous Improvement Process

Given the complexity of a hotel operation and the uniqueness of each guests' needs, a million things can go wrong. In an attempt to get to the fundamental cause of issues that were causing complaints at Hilton, we began reviewing customer complaint verbatim responses, categorizing them, and then ranking them in terms of frequency. While both the employee listening to the complaint and the customer providing the details of the complaint might feel they are in a unique situation, they aren't. Problems not only recur in your operation if you don't fix them, but they are simultaneously occurring in your other locations as well. So, whether you use employees to provide the feedback loop on complaints or analyze customer response data, problem resolution is just the beginning. Once you satisfied the issue with the customer, and hopefully enhanced their loyalty too, the goal should be preventing problems from recurring. Accomplish this by looking into the 'root cause' of the problem; the reason the customer problem occurred in the first place.

Borrowing heavily from Kaizen, W. Edwards Deming, Kaplan & Norton among others (including Sir Francis Bacon's Novum Organum (1620) and Aristotelian logic), we developed a continuous improvement process. It's a plan to determine the root cause, and then correct the underlying issues that create the problem in the first place, so that it doesn't recur.

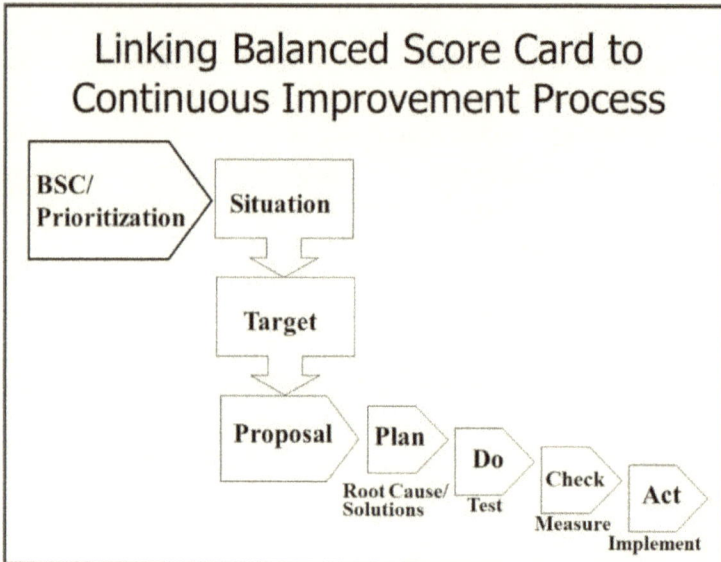

Figure 10-1: The STP/PDCA. A visual representation

In its most basic form, it starts by reviewing performance results obtained from internally gathered data from places like the Balanced Scorecard, survey results, or analysis of customer issues, and then, prioritizing them.

Then, apply the information using the STP process:

Situation: Describe the Situation
Target: Set a Target for Improvement
Proposal: Establish a Proposal that will reach the intended goal

The Proposal becomes the **Plan/Do/Check/Act:**

Plan: Design a plan that creates a solution for the root causes of the problem
Do: Implement the proposed solution to test if it solves the problem
Check: Measure the results of the proposed solution

Act:	If it works, implement the solution. If it doesn't, repeat PDCA.

Now that we've used the STP/PDCA to develop possible solutions to problems that have occurred, what do we do with the solution?

Sharing Service Recovery Results

Customer service recovery is a challenge for some companies, particularly those with multi-unit locations. But even when they do it well, a separate and sometimes more difficult dimensional issue remains. Now that we have found a solution to a customer problem, what is the likelihood that another customer will have the same issue, at this, or another one of your locations?

Creating a 'Best Practices' knowledge bank online or having easy access to one within your unit and among units in multi-location companies is helpful. If you don't have an overall strategic plan for sharing customer solutions, and you have similar customer complaints, potentially you'll need to 'create' a solution 2,500 times if you have 50 employees at each of 50 units. Creating a customer solution feedback mechanism is even more critical, as the ultimate goal of service recovery is to not just solve the problem, but to remove that issue from showing up again. Otherwise, you'll have great customer experiences where you have great customer management leadership, and you won't where you don't. Quarterly best practice contests where employees and business units are encouraged to share their positive service recovery experiences are helpful in expanding a knowledge bank data base. Then, after you've developed a process that captures those 'best practices,' make it easy to access and disseminate system-wide.

But think about it: The GYAN process is more about creating a positive customer experience culture, than about solving individual product or service issues. Yes, it's useful for one-on-one interactions, but to the extent that it permeates the organization, it becomes a GYAN Shared Vision. A vision that creates a customer focused organizational culture, where everyone, every employee, every department, every unit, and your entire global organization work together, creating a loyalty bond with every current and future customer. And, if you're looking for business success, industry leadership, or a sustainable competitive advantage, the GYAN process can help get you there.

Service Recovery and the Loyalty Bond

'What will happen if a Loyal Customer has a problem?'

No one wants something to go wrong during a transaction. And successful companies know that 90+% of their customers have yet to experience a problem. But, as we discussed when we introduced the concept of the loyalty bond in Chapter 5, every customer that hasn't experienced a problem (and even those that have), has an expectation of how they will be treated if a problem was to occur in the future.

Somewhere, hidden in the back of every customer's mind is the question, 'Someday, if/when something goes wrong, how well will it be handled, and what will the company do to make it up to me?' It's their knowledge, belief, or expectation of how they will be treated when something does go wrong. Customers use this evaluation (and their perceived 'leverage'), along with their past experiences and their other expectations, in deciding whether or not to make a future purchase.

Customer loyalty represents a satisfied customer, who will continue to make return purchases, and is willing to be an advocate for your product or service. So, you probably see where I'm going with this. In addition to the current level of service you're providing, if you can get the 90+% of the customers that haven't had a problem, to believe/trust that if they did, that the issue would be resolved to their complete satisfaction, that would have a powerful influence on their current level of loyalty toward your product or service. So, given a loyal customer, add a belief that if a problem were to come up in the future, (or even an issue just as a result in an increase in the customer's future expectations), that their problem would be solved to their complete satisfaction (or that new higher expectations would be met), and you have created a 'Loyalty Bond' with that customer.

In addition, as discussed earlier, this 'Anticipatory Solution Satisfaction' helps distinguish between an ordinary loyal customer, and a loyal customer who not only provides repeat business themselves, but is least likely to defect, and through an actual positive service recovery experience, becomes a *Net Promoter* further encouraging their colleagues to become customers too.

I'm not suggesting that as a general practice that you create problems so you can exceed expectations in resolving them. But from now on, you and your staff should welcome them, as your customers approach you with their complaints. Look at problems and customer complaints as an opportunity to improve and expand the loyalty of your customer base, and move from just 'point in time' loyalty, to a Loyalty Bond.

And when you yourself are a customer somewhere, and you want to test how important customer loyalty is at the place you shop or how much they value you as a customer, try this: Walk in, and say, to the first staff member you see: "I have a complaint," then pause. Gauge their reaction, both verbal and non-verbal. You will be able to quickly determine several things, such as the importance the establishment places on customer loyalty, while getting a glimpse of their customer-oriented culture. You can also learn about the employee: their level of customer training and customer service recovery skills, and whether or not retaining customer's loyalty is a goal for them. And as it relates to you, you'll receive valuable insight, on how important you are as their customer.

And finally, can this higher-level customer 'loyalty bond' be created without a problem having occurred? Definitely. Normally, a loyalty bond exists if the customer has confidence (either through actual experience or through trust) that any problems that might occur, will be resolved to their complete satisfaction. Your service recovery/ resolution process is a key element in creating and maintaining a loyalty bond with your customers.

Recognizing that while customer loyalty is important and is created by a customer's assessment of how likely their expectations will be met the next time, creating a Customer Loyalty Bond operates at an even higher level. This is because in addition to a customer evaluating how things will go the next time, add to this, a customer's knowledge of how things will be handled if things do not go well next time.

So, a customer loyalty bond is created when a loyal customer trusts that their expectations will be met next time *and* any problems that might come up, will be properly resolved to their satisfaction. And that's why problem resolution is so important, because if not handled properly, it not only damages loyalty, but also the loyalty bond expectation they previously may have felt with the company's products or services.

In summary, there is real value in proper problem resolution. If customer expectations are consistently exceeded, it will tend to increase their loyalty. And, if and when problems do occur, and the resolution exceeds the loyal customer's expectations, their 'loyalty bond' can be strengthened as well. Now for an example.

<u>Grocery Store Check Out System Down:</u> Recently, I was at a local chain grocery store. The cashier has just completed the transaction for the customer ahead of me. The customer behind me had not started their transaction. I had just unloaded my groceries onto the checkout conveyor belt. The cashier greeted me and began scanning my items, when the computer system that supported the scanning/check-out process shut down. There was an eerie silence to the normal din of grocery store chatter and scanners beeping. All twelve checkout lines were open, all filled with customers in the middle of their transaction. As the rows of customers stood there, nothing was moving.

Customers began reacting differently, depending on the situation they were in. The customers who just completed their transaction were aware something went wrong, but were free of the problem. They had completed their transaction, so they gathered their bags of groceries and headed out the door.

The customers whose transactions had not started were somewhat more inconvenienced but they still had options. They could choose to wait, their satisfaction with the company then dependent on the speed in which the system and the checkout process re-started. Or they could choose to leave, in which case, they've wasted time shopping and were not able to get the groceries that they had selected, but would not be further inconvenienced. I was stuck. Half of my items were scanned, and the other half were waiting to be scanned, meaning that other similarly situated shoppers in other checkout lanes were also the proverbial 'customer in the middle.' The transaction had started, so we couldn't just leave, but we didn't have any information on when, if ever, the system would restart, so the anxiety level was high and there was no easy solution within sight.

Suddenly, the manager showed up, and on the public-address system announces the following, "This is Ed the store manager. Our computer system has shut down, and at this point in time, I don't know when it will be operational again. I apologize for the inconvenience this has caused you. I'm asking the cashiers to manually bag all groceries that are on the checkout conveyor belt, both items that have been scanned and those that haven't, and give the groceries to the customers, who are then free to leave the store with their groceries, with our apologies." Then he walked by each location, personally apologizing and helped the staff bag scanned and un-scanned items and gave them to us for free.

So, customers in the middle of their transaction, who anticipated either a long wait, or the inconvenience of not getting their groceries, had neither. At the time of the system failure, our expectations were so diminished, we were just hoping to be told the system will be up after a short five-minute wait. But instead of being trapped, we received an apology and a value gesture that exceeded expectations What about the customers in line but no groceries on the belt, or customers in the store still shopping?

They didn't get free groceries, but they too have received something of value that customers rarely get. They have an insight into the 'customer service culture' of the store they've been shopping at. And in so doing, the company created an opportunity to operate in the realm of not just customer loyalty but creating a loyalty bond. I'm sure they are all hoping they are never in a checkout line when the register system goes down, but if they are, they have an increased confidence about how it will be handled, should it happen to them. The result: The store, and its brand, now has a higher perceived value. And not just for those in the store, but also for those who heard about it from their friends. This customer service gesture, probably cost the store $600 at their wholesale cost basis, but the goodwill created will have a positive impact on future customer loyalty for a very long time.

Since that incident, I have increased my spend level at that chain. I still won't drive by too many competitors, but I will seek them out. And it's because of price, selection, and now the competitive advantage they have with me and others in the store that day. While I had been loyal prior to this incident, I had not experienced a problem. Therefore, the 'anticipatory solution satisfaction' question wasn't answered, until now. So, using the terms we've developed, I've moved from customer loyalty to a loyalty bond.

Try to imagine a $600 spend in advertising, discount coupons or special offers having the same impact on future customer loyalty. And, while we're talking about marketing, creating a customer loyalty bond has the potential of reaching the ultimate marketing dream, a 'sustainable competitive advantage.'

Now, had the problem not occurred, estimate the loyalty created by both the absence of the problem and the speedy and friendly checkout of my order. Compare that to the way it was handled when the problem occurred, and ask yourself if the goodwill and customer loyalty created during the problem: decreased, increased, or stayed the same.

This is an example of the power of customer service recovery in terms of giving companies an opportunity to increase customer loyalty and strengthening the loyalty bond to a higher degree, than if the problem had not occurred in the first place. This was a major system failure, but the loyalty bond can be strengthened by tiny issues too. Try this, look for a customer with even a minor problem/ inconvenience, and take that opportunity to exceed service recovery customer expectations and you can positively impact their loyalty bond too.

Customer Value Considerations in Service Recovery

The concept of 'customer value' is important, especially during service recovery when money or value must be returned. Even in enlightened companies that stress making the right 'customer decision,' it's still within the context of 'running a business,' and like any of the thousands of decisions that are made each day, customer decisions need to take the realities of operating a business into consideration.

Determining individual customer value can be useful as a guideline in determining the value of service recovery to invest. If it's to correct a mistake the company made, then do what it takes to correct the mistake. If it's not clear where the mistake was made, I'd rely on the sage advice of Stew Leonard, when he said: "Rule #1 -- The Customer is Always Right"; Rule #2 - If the Customer is Ever Wrong, Re-Read Rule #1."[76]

Give the benefit of the doubt to the customer in the vast majority of situations. The only exception, and it should be extremely rare, is when there is a customer demand that involves a substantial loss of value to the business, such as potential litigation. And, in these rare cases, always escalate before saying no, to the highest level of authority in your organization within your reach.

What about dishonest customers who may not be telling the truth? Use the GYAN process and your creativity to come up with a reasonable solution. Remember, even companies that offer 100% money back service guarantees, still track 'guarantee initiators' to identify customer abuse. What about the chronic 'complainers' and time wasters? You decide. It's always case by case. But when considering letting a customer go unsatisfied, just remember to stay reasonable and flexible.

The correct valuation of the lifetime 'value' should take into account other current and potential new customers that might be impacted, should the current customer issue not be properly resolved. Also keep in mind that you don't always know who the next big value customer will be; not all started out big, and they all don't learn about you or your offerings from your marketing efforts. More and more are learning about your business through current customer referrals, and social media recommendations, (which carry more weight than your advertising). It's always a tough call to let a customer go unsatisfied, and I don't spend much time on the concept of 'getting rid' of customers in this book, but it is part of business reality as well.

Finally, in problem resolution, remember the solution suggested by the customer, may be only one of many possible solutions that will result in a satisfactory conclusion, so use your creativity to develop suggested solutions that yield the highest return. Hopefully, using role playing with the GYAN Process, and the other tools in the book, will help the decision you make, be the correct one.

Chapter Summary

Service Recovery can resolve customer issues that can happen even in the best run organizations. It can also help create a loyalty bond, by setting the expectation that if things do go wrong, they will be resolved to the customer's complete satisfaction. And, as we learned by way of a grocery store example, creative, low cost service recovery can have lasting customer loyalty benefits. The GYAN process can help your employees as well as your managers, operate at the Delight, Surprise and Wow! Levels.

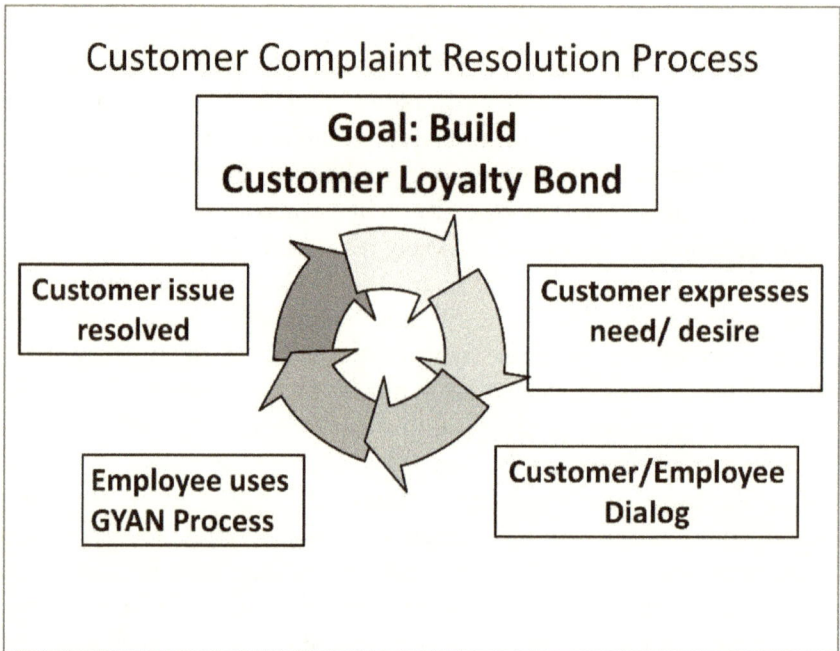

Customer Complaint Resolution Process

Goal: Build Customer Loyalty Bond

Customer issue resolved

Customer expresses need/ desire

Employee uses GYAN Process

Customer/Employee Dialog

Figure 10-2: The Customer Complaint Resolution Process

Conclusion

There are two things that are essential for you to be successful: Knowing 'What' to do, and 'How' to do it.

Customer Dialogue: So you will know 'what' to do

External Market Research: For those pre-customers not yet doing business with you, gather intelligence, through social media or other sources, as you listen to them as they speak individually and collectively in the market places you serve. Listen to what they say about you and your competitors. Listen and learn how their needs are or are not being met, as new wants and needs trends are where your future products and services need to be.

Internal Market Research: Have a process embedded in your business culture to listen to your customers, from the initial contact before the first transaction, to the end of time. It doesn't matter what business you're in, large or small, or if you provide products, services, or both. Listen and observe your customer continuously, pre/in/post transaction, focusing on foundational and experiential wants and needs of customers, both expressed and unexpressed. Use every employee as a listening post and exploit technology as an enabler to listen, anticipate, and respond in real time.

GYAN Process: So you will know 'how' to do it

The 'Give Yourself A Number' process will change the customer and employee culture of your business for the better, if you let it.

But for the GYAN process to have any lasting effect, it has to become part of the thought process for everything your company and your employees do: an enhancement to your culture, not a one-time initiative. It isn't as difficult as it sounds; changing culture, I mean. Make it part of your orientation, your customer interaction training, coaching and mentoring. Make it part of your organization's collective thought process. Use it every time you can, by constantly challenging yourself and your colleagues by saying something like, "that was good; I'd give it a '7'. Let's discuss what an '8' or '9' might be." In my experience with the GYAN process, there is usually an 'ah ha' moment, when employees, one by one, and each on their own personal time-schedule, realize that they really can control the customer experiences and loyalty outcomes. And, like most things that create a new awareness, it permanently changes behavior. You've always told your employees that the customer was important, so directionally, this isn't a new message. Now, you just have to mean it. And do it.

Now It's Up To You

The GYAN process gives everyone the tools, awareness, and the skills that are easily learned. You, (that's everyone reading this, at every level of the organization) just need to live by it, and make it part of everything you do. You just need to decide the difference you and your organization want to make. There are no more excuses. No more vague corporate customer pronouncements, like, "Our customers are our most important asset," that make managers feel they have shown important leadership. It may sound good, to say, but it doesn't provide any real guidance for the employees in their everyday interaction with the customer. And no, customer loyalty no longer depends on the weather, the economy, the competition, technology, the market you're in, etc. It now depends on you.

Once the GYAN process is understood, the 'doing' part is easy. But for it to make a permanent impact and enhance your organization's customer-oriented culture, everyone in the organization must know, support, and practice it.

If your team is frustrated with the various 'flavor of the month' customer and employee initiatives, your HR/Training group will find GYAN is different. If the process is supported from the top, it will not only improve customer loyalty results, but improve employee morale as well. Because now with the GYAN process, instead of trying to avoid providing specific customer service direction because of the complexity and uniqueness of customers, and the multitude of possible situations that make consistent customer specific employee training impossible, you now know not just what to do, at the individual customer level, but how to do it. And as for improving employee morale, you'll also start seeing your employees with a new confidence and sense of conviction, and you might even hear them say, "It really can be done, and now I know how to do it."

I look at life and business as a chess game, filled with challenges, strategy, planning and the goal of winning. In this book, I've tried to provide not just the 'what' and 'why' of customer satisfaction and loyalty, but with the GYAN process, explain the 'how.'

Now, it's your move.

✻ ✻ ✻ ✻ ✻ ✻ ✻ ✻ ✻ ✻ ✻ ✻ ✻ ✻ END ✻ ✻ ✻ ✻ ✻ ✻ ✻ ✻ ✻ ✻ ✻ ✻ ✻ ✻

Appendix

Give Yourself A Number (GYAN) Worksheet Template

Subject: _____

Situation: (Describe):

_____
_____
_____

Your '5' Response (Customer Neutral/Average Response):

_____
_____
_____

Your '1' Response (Customer Negative Response):

_____
_____
_____

Your '10' Response (Best Possible Customer Response):

_____
_____
_____

The Reason for your Response:

_____
_____
_____

Business/Customer Result:

_____
_____
_____

References/Notes

[1] www.gartner.com

[2] The term 'employee' will generally be used throughout the book, representing: team members, internal customers, staff members, associates, workers, partners or whatever you call these valuable people we employ to provide products/services to our customers.

[3] https://research.wpcarey.asu.edu/services-leadership/research/research-initiatives/customer-rage/

[4] https://www.researchgate.net/publication/235357014_Defining_Consumer_Satisfaction

[5] www.hyken.com/customer-loyalty/high-customer-satisfaction-scores-do-not-mean-increased-revenue/

[6] www.accenture.com

[7] Hotel Business News August 7, 2011

[8] http://247wallst.com/special-report/2016/08/23/customer-service-hall-of-fame-4/7/

[9] As mentioned, employees are really 'internal' customers, and are as important as your 'external' customers, and their individual wants and needs are just as complex. The same issues in satisfying external customers exist with employees, and their satisfaction levels should be likewise monitored, measured, and continually improved. Figure out how to satisfy your paying customers, and you'll be well on your way to the insights that lead to solutions for your internal customers as well.

[10] Ballona Wetlands: EPA pollution reduction plan includes 600-acre ecological reserve. (Article: www. argonautnews.com, April 5, 2012

[11] Jeffrey Pfeffer & Robert Sutton: *The Knowing-Doing Gap*. (Harvard Business Press, Boston, MA, 2000).

[12] Reference: www.customerthink.com

[13] "Nordstrom's Employee Handbook Has Only One Rule," article by Ashley Lutz, in *Business Insider*, (Oct. 13, 2014). http://www.businessinsider.com/nordstroms-employee-handbook-2014-10#ixzz3GKLHMKLl

[14] https://www.forbes.com/sites/micahsolomon/2016/01/26/what-any-business-can-learn-from-the-way-nordstrom-handles-customer-service/#29e2494d5b9e

[15] http://frankdiana.wordpress.com/2011/04/10/a-renewed-focus-on-voice-of-the-customer/

[16] "Business Communication Strategies to Overcome Challenges and Influence Listeners." (Praeger, 2010).

[17] (*Hotel Business News*, July 15, 2011).

[18] http://customerthink.com/5-companies-with-envy-worthy-customer-experience.

[19] Notes from *Influencer*, (CD: 2012).

[20] This, according to Ms. Heather Briggs of Hyatt, quoted in an article entitled 'Checking In, After Checkout' by Julie Weed, *The New York Times*, (May 27, 2013)

[21] Often attributed to Peter Drucker, 'what gets measured gets managed.' but others saying similar things include: FW Taylor, WE Deming, and Michael Labeouf, who, in his1985 book 'The Greatest Management Principle in the World' said: "The things that get measured are the things that get done." And don't forget Kaplan and Norton of Balanced Scorecard fame. But, my favorite, is Lord Kelvin who in an 1883 lecture said "I often say that when you can measure what you are speaking about, and express it in numbers, you know something about it; but when you cannot express it in numbers, your knowledge is of a meager and unsatisfactory kind…" http://www.linkedin.com/answers/business-operations/project-management/OPS_PRJ/879407-13138696, wikiquotes.org and others.

[22] *How to Lie with Statistics,* Darrell Huff, Norton, New York, 1954, ISBN 0-393-31072-8.

[23] The concept of Utility, from noted author and management consultant Peter Drucker, who described it this way: "What the customer buys and considers value is never a product. It is always utility, that is, what a product or service does for him."

[24] Source: Jon A. Krosnick, "Response Strategies for Coping with the Cognitive Demands of Attitude Measures in Surveys," *Applied Cognitive Psychology*, (February, 2006).

[25] "6 Ways Google Glass Will Change the Way You Shop," by Matt Brownell, Daily Finance-aol, (Mar 13th 2013 4:27PM).

[26] "Best Western Checks In on Customer Feedback," by Anna Papachristos, *1to1 Magazine*. (Published 05/01/2013)

[27] J.D. Power and Associates, "2012 Social Media Usage Study SM."

[28] Reliability can sometimes be an issue with unqualified or un-restricted access to social media feedback. For example, unscrupulous business owners have been known to write their own positive reviews and non-customers unfamiliar with a product or service can write negative reviews. There have also been agenda driven groups, such as political or unethical organizations, whose members respond as a group to 'trash' a business that doesn't support their particular point of view.

[29] Suheel Sheikh, Chase Branch Manager, Los Angeles, December 2012.

[30] http://travel.usatoday.com/hotels/post/2012/09/best-western-and-wyndham-make-hotel-reviews-easy-to-read/70000989/1?csp=34travel

[31] *J.D. Power and Associates White Paper*, entitled: "Social Media Research Integration in the New Norm." (April 2012)

[32] I've seen occasions where an employee will grant the exception, and then diminish the customer goodwill created, by admonishing the customer that this is a 'one time only' exception. Don't.

[33] *Customers for Life,* by Carl Sewell and Paul B. Brown, (Sep 1, 1990).

[34] http://www.marketwatch.com/story/power-negotiating-after-the-car-warranty-expires-2012-10-20?link=mw_home_kiosk

[35] How small retailers can outgun the big chains, by Dyan Machan, (Sept. 10, 2012\

[36] dennis@giveyourselfanumber.com

[37] *Influencer: The Power to Change Anything,* by Kerry Patterson et al, (2007)

[38] http://humanresources.about.com/od/retention/a/keepnewemployee.htm

[39] It's All About Service: How to Lead Your People to Care for Your Customers, by Ray Pelletier (May 5, 2005)

[40] https://consumerist.com/2016/02/24/best-buy-is-closing-website-to-third-party-sellers-today/

[41] http://hamptoninn3.hilton.com/en/about/index.html

[42] Quote is from a job posting from *Iron mountain* through *Career Builders* 10/22/11 email for Territory Vice President, Cerritos CA.

[43] "It costs 6 – 7 times more to acquire a new customer than retain an existing one." – Bain & Company (*Return on Behavior Magazine*, October 2010)

[44] http://www.brainyquote.com/quotes/quotes/w/wedwardsd131224.html

[45] Question 2 the 'intent to return' question, went through its own evolution. We started by just asking if they intended to return. We found that for many of our hotels, particularly our resorts, these trips were 'once in a lifetime,' hence the revised wording. In addition, as we evaluated the 'return' data, we saw in some cases, the phenomenon of high satisfaction and high advocacy, but low likelihood to return. Turns out, that like those 'once in a lifetime' guests that never plan to return to the location, those that were totally satisfied and were willing to become advocates, when price paid was factored in, didn't feel the price/utility value received was enough for them to re-purchase (they could still recommend). The concept of 'value received' by the customer is obviously important, but could easily be evaluated by the customer and interpreted by the business if needed, by adding a simple 'value received' type question. If they didn't receive 'value' but were satisfied, it was a pricing issue for them, and if they indicated they were advocates, they are generally less price sensitive and may even pay a premium for additional 'value added' services.

[46] Many marketers still confuse 'loyalty' with those seeking 'rewards.' Loyalty denotes, (in addition to satisfaction and frequency), advocacy and an ongoing trust/commitment/belief that the product or service being provided in the future will be at an acceptable level, and therefore it's not just 'points' in a program to offset shortcomings of purchased products/service). So, given our definition of loyalty and the distinctions we've made (high satisfaction, willingness to re-purchase and advocacy), it might be more accurate to call

them 'defection-prevention programs,' or frequency programs, or simply Reward programs, which we'll do, going forward.

[47] As discussed, if the customer is being reimbursed, (like in the case of a business traveler on expense account), the higher cost of a Frequency Program product/service may still be purchased, even if the price premium paid is less than the value of the reward benefit.

[48] http://boardingarea.com/blogs/unroadwarrior/2009/08/23/why-starwood-preferred-guest-is-the-best-loyalty-program/

[49] Recall that basic satisfaction is necessary for Loyalty to exist, but it alone is insufficient, requiring return intent and advocacy to complete our definition.

[50] https://www.linkedin.com/pulse/best-buy-didnt-disaster-proof-its-corporate-algorithms-john-robb

[51] Tropicana, known for its 100% Fresh Squeezed, not from concentrate, orange juice, introduced Trop50®. Its product launch press release, said something similar to: 'This week Tropicana launches Trop50, a breakthrough category innovation delivering the goodness of orange juice with 50 percent less sugar and calories.' How did they accomplish this? They basically diluted their 100% juice with 50% additional water. Here's a customer comment: "'very disappointed.' Don't know about you, but when I buy orange juice from Tropicana, (which I won't be doing ever again, after this), I expect to get actual orange juice. Not "orange juice beverage," which if I had examined the carton more closely I would have realized that was what this new 50% Tropicana Orange Juice actually is. All it is, is watered down orange juice."

[52] www.yelp.com by Lauren E. Tustin, CA, (review: 8/1/11)

[53] *The Ultimate Question-Driving Good Profits and True Growth*, by Fred Reichheld, Harvard Business School Press, (2006).

[54] In my personal experience, in 2018 I was offered a free LA Times Sunday newspaper delivered to my door, probably since a printed newspaper these days is really just a distribution vehicle for advertising print and inserts. As most of the informational 'news' is already available on-line, and is updated in real time, after a few weeks of recycling un-read printed newspapers, I called to cancel my free subscription.

[55] David M. Messick, John M. Darley, and Tom R. Tyler, *Social Influences on Ethical Behavior in Organizations*, Psychology Press (2001).

[56] For further discussion on price fairness, see Maxwell, Sarah: *The Price is Wrong*, New Jersey: John Wiley & Sons, (2008).

[57] Excerpted from: *What's the Difference Between CRM and CEM?* By John Cheney, (Oct. 18, 2013).

[58] Thompson, Ed and Kolsky, Estaban (2004-12-27). "How to Approach Customer Experience Management."

[59] http://www.nielsen.com/us/en/insights/press-room/2012/nielsen-global-consumers-trust-in-earned-advertising-grows.html).

[60] For alternative uses of the term, see Melissa L. Moore, S. Ratneshwar, Robert S. Moore: "Understanding loyalty bonds and their impact on

relationship strength: a service firm perspective," Research Paper: *Journal of Services Marketing,* Vol. 26 Iss: 4, pp.253-264, (2012), Reference: http://www.emeraldinsight.com/journals.htm?articleid=17037060. Their research shows that customers may form different types of loyalty bonds with firms, some that are controllable by the firm, and some which are less controllable. Results provide a starting point for tactical decision making regarding which bonds service providers would like to target in the development of their relationship marketing programs. Also see: *Customer Bonding: Pathway to Lasting Customer Loyalty,* Paperback by Richard Cross and Janet Smith (1996).

[61] http://thinkexist.com/quotes/karl_albrecht/

[62] Before filing for bankruptcy, both <u>Kmart</u> and <u>Circuit City</u> were examples of successful companies in the best seller: *In Search of Excellence.*

[63] "What Science Says about Successful Bosses," Geoffrey James*, www.inc.com,* (2012).

[64] Situational Awareness in this context is more than just knowing where you are and how your reactive mind will robotically respond. It's also being aware and assessing what the customer is saying, doing, experiencing and expecting, before you actually address the need. The GYAN process can help you develop this as a talent.

[65] "How small retailers can outgun the big chains," Doug Fleener, article for *marketwatch.com* (2012).

[66] <u>Strativity Group, Inc.</u> (2009) http://www.strativity.com/products/2009-05-26.aspx

[67] <u>Good Earth Restaurant</u>, Studio City, California on 2/18/11

[68] "Customer Satisfaction is Worthless, Customer Loyalty is Priceless: How to Make Them Love You, Keep You Coming Back, and Tell Everyone They Know," by Jeffrey H. Gitomer (Jun 12, 1998). http://www.amazon.com/Customer-Satisfaction-Worthless-Loyalty-Priceless/product-reviews/188516730X?pageNumber=10

[69] "Between Man and Man," M. Buber: (1st published in 1947).

[70] http://www.wiley.com/WileyCDA/WileyTitle/productCd-0470227540.html

[71] (http://www.usatoday.com/money/industries/travel/2009-06-24-delta-red-coats-service_N.htm)

[72] http://blog.delta.com/2009/06/25/delta-brings-back-red-coats/

[73] http://www.shmula.com/root-causes-of-lost-business-relationships/5411/#fn-5411-1

[74] This was a lesson learned by Netflix, in an article on the impact of their missteps: "The fact is many mildly dissatisfied customers sometimes stick around out of laziness or complacency. Once they're gone, however, they need more than a reinstatement of the status quo to return." http://www.investmentu.com/2011/October/netflix-reverses-dvd-streaming-split.html

[75] An easy way to determine if your organization has a cross-functional service culture is to test the customer service 'hand-off.' See if disparate

departments within an organization have a shared view of the customer, by asking for something from the wrong department intentionally. For example, the next time you stay at a hotel, ask the front desk instead of housekeeping for an extra pillow for your room. Have some fun, and use the GYAN scale to assign a number to the response you get. The response can range anywhere from a 'one': a scowl and an admonition like: "you'll have to get that from the housekeeping department," to a 'ten': I'll have one brought up to your room within the next 5 minutes, and then call you to see if there's anything else you need.'

[76] http://www.stewleonards.com/html/about.cfm

About the Author

Following a successful career with Hilton Hotels Corporation, Dennis Koci is currently available to provide a wide range of Hospitality Consulting services that can easily translate to any company in any industry.

Most recently as Senior Vice President of Operations Support for Hilton Hotels Corporation, he was responsible for the entire corporate functional hotel support division. They included: Customer Loyalty, Front Office, Engineering, Housekeeping, Safety/Security, Communications, Food & Beverage, Technical Services, Human Resources Training and Performance Management.

Koci began his Hilton career in the Front Office of The Palmer House Hilton in Chicago, and prior to joining the corporate staff at Hilton's world headquarters in Beverly Hills in 1986, he served as a General Manager for Hiltons in Los Angeles, Dallas and Hawaii.

In his present role, Koci can assist forward looking organizations create value in key areas such as: Customer Service, Service Recovery, Employee Morale, Loyalty assessments, as well as assist in bringing a Hospitality perspective to the culture of any organization. He can also help improve operational performance through the alignment of the enterprise's strategic direction with the goals of their operating business units, implement improvement initiatives, and guide a company's continuing drive for operational excellence.

He's been a frequent lecturer at academic and hospitality industry venues, (UCLA Hospitality Investment Conference, USC Executive MBA program, WSU, The Conference Board, and The Balanced Scorecard Collaborative), offering perspectives on a wide range of issues from consumer trends and performance management to technology's impact on the hospitality industry.

Koci is a graduate of the University of Illinois – Chicago, where he received a BS Degree in Business Economics, and in 1983 received his MBA from Southern Methodist University – Dallas.

He enjoys photography, chess and competed in the Los Angeles Marathon. He is a credentialed instructor for the state of California, and has taught at California State University, and the University of Hawaii. Koci resides in Los Angeles, California.

www.ingramcontent.com/pod-product-compliance
Lightning Source LLC
Chambersburg PA
CBHW030011290326
41934CB00005B/303